Not Like Us

NOT LIKE US

Immigrants and Minorities in America, 1890–1924

Roger Daniels

The American Ways Series

IVAN R. DEE   *Chicago*

For Judith

with love and gratitude

Library of Congress Cataloging-in-Publication Data:
Daniels, Roger.
    Not like us : immigrants and minorities in America, 1890–1924 / Roger Daniels.
        p.   cm. — (The American ways series)
    Includes bibliographical references and index.
    ISBN: 978-1-56663-166-2 — ISBN 1-56663-166-1
(paper : alk. paper)
    1. Immigrants—United States—History.   2. United States—Emigration and immigration—History.   3. Minorities—United States—History.   4. United States—Race relations.   I. Title.
II. Series.
JV6465.D26   1997
305.895'1073'09034—dc21   97-16117

Contents

Preface

THIS BOOK focuses on struggles over ethnicity and race in late-nineteenth- and early-twentieth-century America, two subjects that are not usually linked in historical writing about the period after 1890. It emphasizes the views of both the dominant majority society and of the minorities, as well as indicating what historians have said about the past. In thus treating the three and a half decades after 1890 as an age of nativism, I do not mean either to negate or to minimize other aspects of that turbulent and dramatic period. I try to place the most important aspects of what can be called, for want of a better term, "minority history" within a framework that indicates the major social, economic, and political concerns of the period. Only within such a context do the historic struggles of Native Americans, African Americans, and various immigrant and ethnic groups become clear.

Most writers on this period stress economics and politics. The 1890s were a major part of what Carl Degler has called the "Age of the Economic Revolution," which transformed the United States from an agrarian to an industrial nation. In that decade the old equilibrium between the two parties dissolved into McKinley Republicanism, which in turn led, in the first decades of the twentieth century, to the Progressive Era, usually seen as the start of an "Age of Reform." This was followed in the 1920s by the overthrow of progressivism in the Harding/Coolidge counterreformation. During the period as a whole, the United States emerged as a world and imperial power and embarked on its first attempts to become one of the prime arbiters of international politics. And, as the following table shows, in the thirty-five years after 1890 more than twenty million immigrants entered the United States—more than in any other comparable period, before or since. How then can this period be treated as an age of nativism?

IMMIGRATION, 1891–1924

Decade	No. of immigrants
1891–1900	3,688,000
1901–1910	8,795,000
1911–1920	5,736,000
1921–1924	2,345,000
Total	20,564,000

Source: INS data

The answer is that by the 1890s powerful anti-immigrant forces had already become organized. Slowly but surely these nativists worked toward what became their major triumph, the so-called National Origins Act of 1924. But it was not just immigrants who were the focus of reactionary forces. The 1890s also mark the last serious attempt by some Northern congressmen to carry out the promises made to African Americans after the Civil War. And, just before 1890, Congress passed "reform" legislation which enabled white developers to get hold of millions of acres of formerly inalienable Indian land.

Nativism—the opposition to all or to certain groups of immigrants—was not new in the 1890s, nor is it merely an American phenomenon. The English writer Daniel Defoe, for example, complained in his essay "True-born Englishman" that "We have become Europe's sink, the Jakes [i.e.,

privy, or toilet] where she voids all her Offal Out-cast prog-
eny." Nativism has been present in America since at least the
mid-eighteenth century when Benjamin Franklin fulminated
against Germans and the German language; in the 1990s it is
alive and well in a number of places. Today in the United
States, where most often the targets are speakers of Spanish; in
Canada where it is most often Chinese who are complained of;
in Germany and Austria where the "others" are usually Bosni-
ans or Turks; and in France where the resented ones are
usually North Africans, immigration has become what com-
mentators call a "hot-button" topic. Contemporary right-wing
political leaders such as Pat Buchanan in the United States,
Jörg Haider in Austria, and Jean Le Pen in France have tried
to vault themselves into power by attacking immigrants as job
stealers and destroyers of culture.

Two distinct periods of American nativism preceded the
one described in this book. The end of the eighteenth century
saw a short-lived, politically motivated attack on radical
immigrants from Ireland and France, culminating in the infamous Alien and Sedition Acts of John Adams's administration. More seriously, in the 1850s political nativists in the
Know Nothing movement actually formed a political party—
the American party—and ran a candidate for president.
Their targets were Catholics of any description but particularly Irish and German immigrant Catholics. The Civil War
sounded the death knell of the Know Nothing movement as it
became clear, on the one hand, that the most subversive group
in American life was composed of native-born Americans
who would destroy the Union, and, on the other, that ethnic
soldiers and regiments were strong supporters of the nation.
Perhaps nothing better exemplifies the positive attitude toward immigrants held by the Civil War Congresses than the

fact that the Homestead Act of 1862 gave immigrants who had declared their intention to become citizens the same rights as citizens themselves.

Although the causes of the Civil War are complex and much debated, many historians agree with Abraham Lincoln that slavery "somehow" caused the war. In the aftermath of war three constitutional amendments—the Thirteenth (1865), Fourteenth (1868), and Fifteenth (1870)—abolished slavery, made the former slaves citizens, and made it illegal for anyone to be denied the vote because of race, color, or previous condition of servitude. But it took more than a few strokes of the pen to end the effects of two and a half centuries of slavery. For a time, just after the war, many Northern politicians seemed determined to create a social revolution in the South and to do so with army bayonets if necessary. But few finally had the stomach for it. By the time the narrative of this book begins, most Southern blacks had been abandoned by their Northern protectors, and the white South was relatively free to violate the Fifteenth Amendment and otherwise contravene both the letter and spirit of the Constitution.

For many American Indian tribes the Civil War provided a brief respite from the incursions of white settlers with military protection into their narrowing but still considerable domains. Whites, of course, tended to regard those domains as what Frederick Jackson Turner called "unoccupied territory." The end of the war, the Homestead Act, and, above all, the construction of transcontinental railroads, starting with the Union Pacific and Central Pacific, completed at Promontory Point, Utah, in May 1869, all presaged accelerated white settlement on Indian lands. Despite an occasional victory, such as Crazy Horse and Sitting Bull's triumph over the rash General Custer at the Little Bighorn in July 1876, the twenty-five years following the Civil War put an end to the freedom of the

Plains Indians. It was in these years that Indian reservations—first introduced by Americans in California in the 1850s—became the home of the once-free Lakota, Arapahoe, Nez Perce, and other peoples of the Great Plains and the mountain West.

Nothing better prefigured what was to happen to native Americans, African Americans, and most immigrants in the quarter-century after 1890 than the experience of the Chinese, the first numerically significant group of free immigrants of color to come to the United States. Thus an initial examination of the early decades of the Chinese-American experience will provide a good introduction to what was to come.

This book was written during a wanderjahr in Germany, Austria, and Canada, and I have debts of all kinds to acknowledge. At Halle, Innsbruck, and Calgary, my hosts, Professor Hans-Jürgen Grabbe, University Professor Brigitte Scheer, and Dean Stephen J. Randall created conditions that made creative work simple, as did their staffs. I received particularly helpful research assistance from Paul Chastko at Calgary. While I was away, my Cincinnati research assistant, now Dr. Andrew Kersten, was efficient in supplying materials not available abroad. I also thank my department head and dean at Cincinnati, Gene Lewis and Joe Caruso, who have facilitated and supported my travel and scholarship in many ways. The draft manuscript benefited greatly from a vigorous reading by John Braeman. The publisher, Ivan R. Dee, provided good counsel and meticulous editing. Finally and chiefly, I thank my fellow traveler, Judith, who edits and improves everything I do. Despite these many accomplices, I alone am responsible for any errors of commission or omission.

Not Like Us

Prologue: Chinese Exclusion, 1882

WE DO NOT KNOW when the first Chinese came to the New World. A few came to Mexico as early as the sixteenth century aboard Spain's fabled Manila galleons. Similarly we cannot be sure about the first Chinese in the United States. Almost certainly they were seamen left in American ports in the late eighteenth century. Numerically meaningful immigration of Chinese into the United States began at about the time of the California gold rush in 1849; the hundreds and then thousands of Chinese men who flocked to San Francisco were drawn by the same gold fever that drew even larger numbers of other migrants to California. The Chinese characters for California can also mean "gold mountain," and in the Cantonese dialect a person who emigrated to California was a *gamsaanhaak* or "Gold Mountain guest." Many, perhaps most of the immigrants intended to work for a time in California and then return to China as "rich" men. Some actually did so, but most of those who survived remained poor and became settlers rather than sojourners, as did large numbers of nineteenth-century male immigrants from Europe who came to California with the same intention.

These Gold Mountain guests were part of a much larger Chinese diaspora that had begun centuries earlier with large-scale voluntary Chinese emigration into Southeast Asia, the area Chinese call Nanyang. As early as 1806, well before the abolition of the African slave trade, Westerners, led by the British, created the so-called coolie trade which transported hundreds of thousands of Asians, mostly Chinese and Asian

Indians, as indentured laborers to plantations all over the tropical and semitropical world. One of its historians, Hugh Tinker, described the trade, aptly, as "a new system of slavery." In the New World Chinese immigrant workers, largely coolies, played major economic roles in the Caribbean, Peru, and Hawaii, as did free Chinese immigrants in the North American West. Except in North America, the production of sugar absorbed most of their labor.

An investigatory commission set up by the Chinese government in the 1870s concluded that "of the [150,000] Chinese labourers who have proceeded to Cuba, 8 or 9 of every 10 have been conveyed there against their will." The conditions under which the Chinese worked in Cuba can only be described as barbaric: Robert L. Irick's judgment that "nothing in the slave trade literature reads worse than the accounts of maltreatment in Cuba" is surely overstated, but not by much. Most of the 88,000 Chinese who were brought to Peru between 1849 and 1875 worked on sugar and cotton plantations, but a particularly wretched minority, perhaps a fifth and all male, were put to tasks on Peru's guano islands. One contemporary Peruvian newspaper reported that "The greatest part of those being newly contracted by the plantations are coming to replace, not those who are completing their contracts, but rather those who died fulfilling them."

The initial movement of Chinese laborers to Hawaii was a minor part of the coolie trade. The first cargo of 180 coolies was imported into Hawaii in 1852 by the newly founded Royal Hawaiian Agricultural Society, one of whose purposes was to introduce "coolie labor from China to supply the places of the rapidly declining native population." In that year the governor of Hong Kong, Sir John Bowring, described the procedures in the holding pens on the China coast where the laborers were kept, under guard, until their ships came: "I have myself seen the arrangements for the shipment of coolies at Amoy; hundreds of them gathered together in barracoons, stripped naked, and stamped or painted with the letter C (Cuba), P (Peru), or S (Sandwich Islands) on their breasts."

Those brought to Hawaii were bound by contract to serve for five years at three dollars a month plus food, clothing, and shelter. While servitude in Hawaii seems not to have been quite as brutal as in the Caribbean or Peru, it was servitude in an oligarchy dominated by white, largely American plantation owners. A few Chinese, peddlers and merchants, had preceded the laborers to the islands, the first being reported in Honolulu in 1823. The census of 1853 reported 123 Chinese men and no Chinese women living in Honolulu in addition to the workers on the plantations. All told, some 46,000 Chinese contract laborers came to Hawaii before American annexation in 1898 brought the islands under the jurisdiction of U.S. law which both outlawed contract labor and prohibited further Chinese labor immigration.

The 250,000 Chinese who came to the United States between 1849 and 1882 were neither contract laborers nor coolies; they were immigrants who came by choice—though, to be sure, many if not most of them were in debt to other Chinese for their passage money in a credit ticket system. Evidence from the 1850s speaks of a $70 advance ($50 for the ticket and $20 for expenses); the emigrant was expected to pay back $200. The Chinese who came to the American West were pulled by a much higher standard of living and a relative shortage of labor. The immigrants were overwhelmingly (more than 90 percent) male and almost exclusively from the Pearl River Delta of Guangdong Province, a traditional area of emigration. Although Chinese immigration was predominantly of male laborers, some women, merchants, political exiles, and students also came. A large number, perhaps a majority, of the Chinese women were prostitutes, many of them "slave girls" coerced into the trade against their will. As late as 1880 there were fewer than 5,000 Chinese women in the United States. The most famous student, Yung Wing, came to the United States in 1847, was graduated from Yale College in 1854, married a white American woman, and is the author of the first Asian-American autobiography. This table shows the number of Chinese recorded in late-nineteenth-century censuses, their gender and citizenship.

CHINESE AMERICAN POPULATION, SEX,
CITIZENSHIP, AND SEX RATIO, 1860–1930

Year	Male	Female	Total	Ratio	Citizen	Alien
1860	33,149	1,784	34,933	18.6:1	n/a	n/a
1870	58,633	4,566	63,199	12.8:1	n/a	n/a
1880	100,686	4,779	105,465	21.1:1	n/a	n/a
1890	103,620	3,868	107,488	26.8:1	n/a	n/a
1900	85,341	4,522	89,863	18.9:1	9,010	80,853
1910	66,858	4,675	71,531	14.3:1	14,935	56,596
1920	53,891	7,748	61,639	7.0:1	18,532	43,107
1930	59,802	15,152	74,954	3.9:1	30,868	44,086

Source: U.S. Census data

Throughout the later nineteenth century more than 90 percent of Chinese Americans lived in the ten westernmost states, more than two-thirds of them in California. Chinese workers engaged in mining, cleared land, and pioneered in agriculture in the underdeveloped American West. Perhaps most significant, they were crucial in the construction of Western railroads. Just as Irish immigrant labor had been largely responsible for digging canals and building railroads in the eastern United States, Chinese did much of the construction of

Western railroads in the United States and Canada. Most spectacular was their work on the first transcontinental railroad, including the difficult and highly dangerous dynamiting of a right-of-way through the high Sierras in California and Nevada. When that road was completed at Promontory Point, Utah, perhaps ten thousand Chinese workers were discharged; most of them found their way back to San Francisco where their presence in a depressed labor market helped an existing and virulent anti-Chinese movement gain strength in the late 1860s.

With its roots in San Francisco, the anti-Chinese movement quickly spread to other parts of California, the West, and the nation. Based on the economic opposition of organized workingmen to "cheap Chinese labor," it had, from its inception, a thoroughly racist character, as did the "pro-Chinese" arguments of employers and their spokesmen. The use of Chinese strikebreakers in a well-publicized shoemakers' strike in North Adams, Massachusetts, in 1870 crystallized existing anti-Chinese sentiments among Eastern labor leaders. For example, John Swinton, an important New York labor editor, wrote in 1870 that Chinese were an "inferior type" of humanity, bringing paganism, incest, sodomy, and the threat of miscegenation to American shores. Not just workingmen held such racist attitudes; they were endemic in American society. Caleb Cushing, a member of the Northern elite who was American commissioner to China in the 1840s, voiced sentiments which exemplified both American racism and the attitude that justified American imperialism.

> [We belong] to the excellent white race, the consummate impersonation of intellect in man and loveliness in woman, whose power and privilege it is, wherever they may go . . . to Christianize and civilize, to command and to be obeyed, to conquer and to reign. I admit to an equality with

me . . . the white man—my blood and race, whether he be
a Saxon of England, or the Celtic of Ireland. But I do not
admit as my equals either the red man of America, or the
yellow man of Asia or the black man of Africa.

In San Francisco the movement was led by the sandlot agi-
tator Dennis Kearney, himself a recent immigrant from Ireland. Its simplistic slogan, "The Chinese must GO!,"
disguised the movement's real goal: halting Chinese immigration. Although Chinese laborers were thought necessary by
entrepreneurs such as the railroad builder Charles Crocker, an
anti-Chinese consensus soon developed in California and the
West which was embraced by all shades of political opinion.

Even before the movement against them became politically
significant, Chinese in California were subjected to many
kinds of special mistreatment. Three factors made their experience unique: their race, the underdeveloped region to which
they came, and the variety of discriminations they encountered. In the now notorious case of *People v. Hall* (1854), the
California Supreme Court ruled that the testimony of Chinese
against white persons could not be accepted in court. (Similar
laws existed in many states about the testimony of American
Indians and slaves.) The practical effect of this ruling was to
make Chinese the ideal targets of criminals, anti-Chinese
mobs, and hooligans generally: the victims could not effectively complain to what little law enforcement there was in
post-gold-rush California. No wonder the newly coined
phrase "a Chinaman's chance" meant no chance at all. No one
will ever know how many Chinese were murdered in late-
nineteenth-century America, but hundreds were killed by
mobs from Los Angeles to New York City, and many others
were slain by individuals. Although most of the slayers of Chinese went unpunished, in California at least two whites were

convicted of such murders, though one of the convictions was reversed on appeal.

A further major legal distinction was created in 1870 when the U.S. Congress rewrote the naturalization laws. The original 1790 statute limited naturalization to "free white persons," the intent being to deny citizenship to African Americans, free or slave, and indentured servants of any color. Under any reading of the law, Chinese and other Asians were ineligible, but in fact American courts had naturalized a few Chinese and Japanese. The ending of slavery, the adoption of the Fourteenth Amendment, the philosophy of Radical Reconstruction, and the scheme of some Republican politicians to create a black Republican electorate in the South made the old naturalization law inappropriate. Senator Charles Sumner, the radical Republican from Massachusetts, and a few others in Congress sought to make the new naturalization law color-blind and universal. But a large majority in both houses, its anti-Chinese consciousness having been raised, rejected Sumner's egalitarianism and amended the law so that naturalization was limited to white persons—the word "free" was dropped—and to "aliens of African nativity and to persons of African descent."

Four years earlier, when Congress had approved the text of what became the Fourteenth Amendment, no such anti-Chinese consciousness had existed. That amendment's first words—"All persons born or naturalized in the United States . . . are citizens of the United States and the state wherein they reside"—established for the first time a national citizenship. Adopted in 1868, it, plus the naturalization statute enacted two years later, created the anomalous situation that while children of Asian immigrants born in the United States were full citizens, their parents, alone of all other races and ethnic groups, were barred from becoming naturalized citizens.

A wide variety of state and territorial statutes and local ordinances were created to persecute Chinese throughout the American West. The most significant kind of statute barred Chinese in many states and territories from participating in mining, which had been one of their most important sources of income. Local ordinances, particularly in San Francisco where about a quarter of all Chinese Americans lived, harassed their businesses—for example, Chinese laundries were taxed higher than other laundries—and attacked their way of life. A San Francisco "anti-queue" ordinance, for example, required cutting off the long braids of hair that Chinese law required men to wear. (Many such laws were ultimately declared unconstitutional by both state and federal judges.) A specifically anti-Chinese section was written into California's new 1879 constitution, forbidding public bodies from employing Chinese and calling upon the legislature to protect "the state . . . from the burdens and evils arising from" their presence. That year a statewide anti-Chinese referendum passed by 154,638 to 883 (99.4 percent). The Western anti-Chinese movement was not something invented by politicians: in the words of the pioneer labor historian Lucille Eaves, it "sprang from the people."

But to effect what the vast majority of Californians wanted—an end to Chinese immigration—action by Congress was needed. This was because the so-called commerce clause of the Constitution placed control of foreign and interstate commerce in Congress's hands, and the Supreme Court had ruled in the *Passenger Cases* of 1849 that immigration was foreign commerce. The grant of power to Congress preempted the ability of states to regulate immigration, even though Congress had not legislated. It took about a dozen years—from 1870 to 1882—of sustained anti-Chinese agitation before the desired congressional legislation was passed and enacted.

There were a number of obstacles: the unwillingness of many in Congress to bring federal power to bear in a new field, immigration; the traditional pro-immigration stance of the Republican party—as the 1864 GOP platform put it, "foreign immigration . . . should be fostered and encouraged"; the fact that most of the country did not care about Chinese immigration; the lobbying of two interest groups, merchants and missionaries, each of which feared that anti-Chinese action in America would adversely affect their efforts in China; and, more specifically, the 1868 Burlingame Treaty between the United States and China, which had established the reciprocal right of Americans and Chinese to migrate to each other's country. Both countries had also pledged to eliminate the coolie trade. The treaty, whose major purpose was to promote trade, put immigration policy and foreign policy at loggerheads. The text of the treaty contains perhaps the most sweeping endorsement of immigration in American law, and one from which the United States quickly retreated: ". . . the United States of America and the Emperor of China cordially recognize the inherent and inalienable right of man to change his home and allegiance, and also the mutual advantage of the free migration and emigration of their citizens and subjects respectively from one country to the other for purposes of curiosity, of trade or as permanent residents."

When President Ulysses S. Grant sent Congress a message in 1874 suggesting that the body do something about Chinese immigration, he began a long series of presidential statements opposing Chinese immigration. No American president before Franklin D. Roosevelt said anything favorable about Chinese immigration, though most were somewhat inhibited in

their denunciations of the "evil" by notions of national interest. Grant's message and much congressional debate produced
the first statute in American history that restricted nonslave
immigration. The 1875 law, known as the Page Act, made it a
crime for Americans to participate in the "cooly-trade,"
barred the entry of persons under sentence for nonpolitical offenses, of persons whose sentence had been remitted on condition of emigration, and of women "imported for the purpose
of prostitution." Although no enforcement bureaucracy was
created, and federal courts insisted on proof that women were
actually prostitutes, it is clear that the law made it difficult for
Chinese women to enter the country and probably deterred
some from even trying. This minor act was the start of modern American immigration restriction. It also marked the introduction of what would become a minor motif in
anti-immigrant legislation: the notion that immigrants, and
especially immigrant women, were contaminating pure and
innocent American men.

The next year, an election year, Congress set up a joint congressional committee to investigate Chinese immigration.
Three senators and two representatives, including two Californians who were committed "anti-coolieites," traveled to
San Francisco and heard several days of testimony from persons representing a wide spectrum of Western opinion. That
testimony showed clearly the class nature of the opposition to
Chinese. Businessmen, large-scale agriculturalists, and some
religious leaders opposed restrictions against Chinese; most
other Californians, and the politicians who depended upon
their votes, favored them. The arguments of the former
groups stressed the economic value of Chinese labor and the
damage to American interests abroad that anti-Chinese action
in America might trigger. One missionary, the Reverend Otis
Gibson, did speak of what we would today call "human

rights" and invoked the spirit of the Declaration of Independence. The arguments of the opponents of Chinese immigration were both economic and cultural: the "Chinaman," most proponents of restriction insisted, "worked cheap and smelled bad."

Back in Washington in 1877 the committee recommended restriction, though its chair, Republican Senator Oliver P. Morton of Indiana, issued a minority report pointing to the racism that motivated the committee's action and insisting that "if the Chinese in California were white people, being in all other respects what they are, I do not believe that the complaints and warfare made against them would have existed to any considerable extent." Although numerous anti-Chinese bills were dropped into the congressional hoppers, none was acted upon positively until the so-called Fifteen Passenger Bill of 1879 passed both houses. It would have limited to fifteen the number of Chinese on a single vessel bound for the United States, but President Rutherford B. Hayes vetoed the measure. His veto message assured Congress that diplomatic negotiations with China to revise the Burlingame Treaty were in progress, which should clear the way for congressional action that he could approve. A new 1880 treaty with China gave the United States the right to "regulate, limit or suspend" the immigration of Chinese laborers.

The Chinese issue was thought important enough in the 1880 presidential election for some Democratic dirty-tricksters to forge the so-called Morey letter, in which GOP presidential nominee James A. Garfield expressed "pro-Chinese" sentiments. In fact, both Democrats and Republicans had adopted anti-Chinese planks in their political platforms, and some kind of federal anti-Chinese legislation seemed a foregone conclusion in the next session of Congress.

Congress acted in 1881. Using the language of the 1880

Sino-American treaty, it passed a bill suspending the immigration of Chinese laborers for twenty years. President Chester A. Arthur vetoed this bill, insisting in his message that "a shorter experiment" was wiser. Congress then enacted a ten-year suspension, which Arthur signed on May 6, 1882. Although officially titled the "Chinese Exclusion Act," the law permitted the entrance of certain Chinese: teachers, students, merchants, and "travellers for pleasure." It also specifically barred Chinese persons from naturalization, though the 1870 naturalization law had already effected that without specifically mentioning Chinese. Between 1882 and the repeal of Chinese exclusion in 1943, American immigration records show that nearly 95,000 Chinese entered legally, an annual average of about 1,500.

Some Chinese and their lawyers fought what they considered an unjust law by challenging the Exclusion Act in the courts. But Justice Stephen J. Field, a Californian who had handed down a number of opinions upholding Chinese-American property rights, spoke for the Supreme Court in the Chinese Exclusion Case and ruled the law constitutional: "[If Congress] considers the presence of foreigners of a different race in this country, who will not assimilate with us, to be dangerous to its peace and security, . . . its determination is conclusive on the judiciary." The ban was extended for a further ten years in 1892, and the act was made "permanent" in 1902.

All the laws and parts of laws that excluded Chinese were repealed at Franklin D. Roosevelt's request in 1943 as a gesture to a wartime ally. Today Chinese exclusion is all but universally regarded as an unfortunate mistake. For several generations, however, it was generally believed to be a necessary expedient. In 1922, for example, the progressive labor historian Selig Perlman could write: "The anti-Chinese agitation in California, culminating as it did in the Exclusion

Law passed by Congress in 1882, was doubtless the most important single factor in the history of American labor, for without it the entire country might have been overrun by Mongolian labor and the labor movement might have become a conflict of races instead of one of classes."

The passage of the Chinese Exclusion Act had far-reaching effects. Its initial impact, of course, was felt chiefly by the Chinese-American community. Its growth was cut off, its structure frozen. As the table on page 6 shows, the Chinese-American population declined steadily from the 1880s [there was probably an intercensal population peak of perhaps 125,000 in 1882] to the 1920s. The long persistence of a heavily male sex ratio, characteristic of the early stages of migration, is unique in the history of American ethnic groups. Thus the Chinese-American community was an aging one. In 1920, for example, 35.6 percent of Chinese males were over fifty years of age, and the median male Chinese age was forty-two years. Chinese females, on the other hand, predominantly native born, were a young population. Nearly 70 percent were under thirty years of age, and their median age was nineteen years. Such a population, in which there were few women and families and always more older men than younger ones, was not likely to be as receptive to acculturation as were most other immigrant communities. The largely bachelor society that dominated Chinese America until after World War II was highly conservative.

Although Chinese Americans remained predominantly Westerners, they dispersed considerably. By 1940 a bare majority, 51 percent, lived in California, and 60.4 percent lived in the ten westernmost states. New York City was home to more than twelve thousand Chinese, more than in all the Western states other than California combined, and another three thousand lived in Chicago and Boston. After 1880 increasing numbers of Chinese lived in large cities and engaged in urban pursuits. Chinese-owned laundries and restaurants—labor-intensive businesses requiring little capital—employed more and more of them. While some laundries were family-owned and -operated, like the one described in Maxine Hong Kingston's marvelous book *The Woman Warrior*, others employed large numbers of single men at minimal wages and under abominable working conditions. From the very first there were successful Chinese entrepreneurs, and the wealthiest merchants in cities such as San Francisco, New York, and Seattle were as well off as all but the richest Gilded Age magnates.

After the passage of the Exclusion Act, many Chinese became the first voluntary illegal immigrants in American history. Chinese not only crossed the borders illegally and jumped ship, they also took advantage of a natural disaster and American law to perpetrate an elaborate immigration fraud: the so-called "paper sons" scam. The great San Francisco earthquake and fire of 1906 destroyed the Bay City's vital statistics records. Under American law, native-born Chinese who returned to China and fathered children there could bring the children—but not their alien mothers—into the United States. Those who had successfully established American citizenship often sold the "slots" that their trips to China created, or they brought in cousins or other kinsmen rather than sons. It is clear that large numbers of the male citizens recorded in the census were paper sons. For example, the 1930 census recorded 20,693 male Chinese-American citizens and only 10,175 females in that category. Under normal conditions the numbers should have been roughly equal. Community members are now willing to talk about the fraud. As one paper son told Victor and Brett de Bary Nee:

In the beginning my father came in as a laborer. But the 1906 earthquake came along and destroyed all those immigration things. So that was a big chance for a lot of Chinese. They forged themselves certificates saying that they were born in this country, and when the time came they could go back to China and bring back four or five sons just like that! They might make a little money off it, not much, but the main thing was to bring a son or a nephew or a cousin in.

The Chinese Exclusion Act, usually treated by historians as an unfortunate minor incident, was much more than that. It affected not only Chinese; it became the hinge on which all American immigration policy turned. Before the passage of the act there had been no effective exclusion of aliens except for reasons of disease, and that exclusion was implemented by local health and police authorities. Nor had there been any deportation of aliens: not even one individual had been formally deported by the Aliens Act signed by John Adams in 1798, and no other deportation statute existed. The exclusion of most Chinese in 1882 ended the era of free and unrestricted access to the United States. Although the volume of immigration continued to grow steadily until the outbreak of World War I, so did anti-immigration legislation. And in the post–World War I era, major immigration legislation greatly narrowed the opening in the so-called golden door.

In addition, if immigration was to be restricted, a federal immigration bureaucracy had to be created to enforce it. Chinese exclusion thus was a factor in helping convince Congress to add to the repressive powers of the federal government. And, as students of constitutional and immigration law know well, those powers were first tested in a variety of cases brought by Chinese and their lawyers. Charles and Laurene McClain have pointed out that, although the Chinese who went to court were interested primarily in getting results favorable to themselves, "the willingness of Chinese litigants to confront the government in a succession of cases gave rise to sharper delineations of limits on governmental authority and the rights of citizens and noncitizens. In defining these limits and rights, they contributed far more to the ideals of democracy and republicanism upon which their adopted country was based than did their antagonists." To be sure, these cases did not change the anti-Chinese character of American law, but they did ensure that many Chinese at least received due process or something close to it. As there was no system of appellate law in China, the widespread use of the courts by Chinese in the United States was a clear indication that members of this "unassimilable race" could adapt to American conditions.

Even though we have no reliable public opinion polls before the late 1930s, it is clear that Chinese exclusion had the support of the overwhelming majority of Americans. Even John Marshall Harlan, the late-nineteenth-century Supreme Court justice whose dissents in civil rights cases set him apart from his fellow justices, had no respect for Chinese. In a family letter he wrote favorably of the Chinese Exclusion Act and noted that the American people would not welcome "a tide of immigration [of] Asian savages." He assumed the Chinese would not assimilate. Only Americans, he argued, "or those who become such by long stay here, understand American institutions." As far as Chinese were concerned, the great dissenter merely concurred with the views of most other Americans.

But opinion was clearly divided about restricting other kinds of immigrants. The following quotations, all from Baptist ministers in the 1880s, can be considered as a kind of dialogue about immigration. The first two represent the more traditional optimistic view while the third prefigures the pessimism and loss of confidence more typical of the 1890s and beyond.

In 1883 the Reverend John Peddie of New York City proclaimed to Europe, in words strikingly similar to those of Emma Lazarus later emblazoned on the Statue of Liberty: "Send us your poor and degraded you would trample underfoot and on our wide plains and prairies, under the fostering light of our free institutions, of education, and religion, we will make out of them such noble specimens of manhood as never grew on your cramped and narrow soil."

While Peddie saw America as the savior of immigrants, two years later the Baptist Home Missionary Society went so far as to see immigrants as the savior of America, declaring that "as the barbarians that swept down upon the Roman Empire infused fresh blood into the decaying Latin race, so these immigrants are bringing to us a brawn that will help save the native American stock from physical deterioration."

But in 1888, Professor E. H. Johnson of Crozier Theological Seminary struck a note of alarm that would echo for the next few decades:

> I have stood near Castle Garden [the New York immigrant depot before Ellis Island was opened in 1892] and seen races of far greater peril to us than the Irish. I have seen the Hungarians, and the Italians and the Poles. I have seen these poor wretches trooping out, wretches physically, wretches mentally, wretches morally, and stood there almost trembling for my country, and said, what shall we do if this thing keeps on? In the name of God, what shall we do if the American race is to receive constant influx of that sort of thing?

1

The United States in the Grey Nineties

ALTHOUGH Hollywood and other merchants of nostalgia have long perpetrated the myth of a Gay Nineties, a genteel and relaxed era, the 1890s were in fact one of the most turbulent and stressful decades in American history. They were scarred by the worst depression the United States had experienced to that time and witnessed the deterioration of racial and ethnic relations. Toward their close there occurred one of the great realignments in domestic political history. In foreign affairs the decade marked the beginnings of an American overseas empire largely as the result of a "splendid little war" that is now more likely to be regarded as shameful or sordid.

Many historians have regarded the decade as an important nodal point in the American past, a time when one era ended and another began. The first of these was Frederick Jackson Turner, who in 1893 produced the most famous and influential essay ever written by an American historian. The young University of Wisconsin professor drew on the highly positive report of the superintendent of the census for 1890 which began:

> This census completes the history of a century; [i.e., since the first census of 1790] a century of progress and achievement unequaled in the world's history. . . . It has witnessed . . . the spread of settlement across the continent until not less than 1,947,280 square miles have been brought into the service of man. . . .

Many pages later the superintendent noted that "Up to and including 1880 the country had a frontier of settlement, but at present the unsettled area has been so broken into by isolated bodies of settlement that there can hardly be said to be a frontier line."

It was this sentence, not at all emphasized in the report, that Turner used as a launching pad for his famous frontier thesis which linked the existence of free land to the development of democratic institutions, what some have called yeoman democracy:

> The existence of an area of free land, its continuous recession, and the advance of American settlement westward, explain American development. . . . And now, four centuries from the discovery of America, at the end of a hundred years of life under the Constitution, the frontier has gone, and with its going has closed the first period of American history.

Turner's argument implied that for the foreseeable future a chief problem for the United States would be how to maintain American democracy when its presumed source, that "area of free land," and the ways of life it imposed on its settlers, no longer existed. In an essay published two years later, the Wisconsin historian wrote that "it is the fact of unoccupied territory in America that sets the evolution of American and European institutions at contrast." Turner thus transformed a

typically self-congratulatory census report into an elegy for a
world Americans had lost.

More than a half-century later, another historian, Henry
Steele Commager, wrote in an essentially celebratory manner
of "the watershed of the nineties," arguing that the decade
marked the birth of modern America:

> As with all watersheds the topography is blurred, but in the
> perspective of half a century the grand outlines emerge
> clearly. On the one side lies an America predominantly
> agricultural; concerned with domestic problems; conform-
> ing, intellectually at least, to the political, economic, and
> moral principles inherited from the seventeenth and eigh-
> teenth centuries—an America still in the making, physi-
> cally and socially; an America on the whole self-confident,
> self-contained, self-reliant, and conscious of its unique
> character and of a unique destiny. On the other side lies the
> modern America, predominantly urban and industrial; in-
> extricably involved in world economy and politics; troubled
> with the problems that had long been thought peculiar to
> the Old World; experiencing profound changes in popula-
> tion, social institutions, economy, and technology; and try-
> ing to accommodate its traditional institutions and habits of
> thought to conditions new and in part alien.

Contemporaries too were aware of the crucial nature of the
decade. At the 1892 convention of the Populist party, one of
its key spokesmen, Ignatius Donnelly, showed that he, like
Turner, felt that American democracy was endangered. But
Donnelly's fears came not from the disappearance of the West
but from the dominance of the East. In his preamble to the
Populist platform he complained that

> we meet in a nation brought to the verge of moral, political,
> and material ruin. Corruption dominates the ballot-box,
> the Legislatures, the Congress, and even touches the er-

mine of the bench. The people are demoralized. . . . The urban workmen . . . are rapidly degenerating into European conditions. . . . From the same prolific womb of government injustice we breed the two great classes—tramps and millionaires.

While Donnelly's remarks are obviously hyperbole, they do indicate the serious economic dislocations that accompanied the massive industrial growth of late-nineteenth-century America, a growth that accompanied what many economic historians have dubbed the second industrial revolution. The first industrial revolution had been centered in Great Britain in the latter decades of the eighteenth century; its key element was steam power fueled at first largely by water and then by coal. The second industrial revolution of the latter decades of the nineteenth century was centered in the United States and Germany; it featured a wave of innovations in the production of metals and other materials, machinery, chemicals, and foodstuffs; after the 1880s it was increasingly powered by electricity.

In the United States the effects of the first industrial revolution had altered the direction and hastened the growth of the American economy, especially after 1800. In addition, the changes it wrought in Europe both increased the "push" factors that led to mass migrations of Europeans overseas—largely to the United States—and created mass urban markets for American foodstuffs and fibers. Their export provided much of the capital for American growth. The effects of the second industrial revolution transformed the United States into a modern urban nation with the largest economy in the world. By the 1890s, though the export of foods and fibers continued to be important, the United States was for the first time exporting more manufactured goods than it was importing. Andrew Carnegie, the Scots immigrant boy who dominated the American steel industry, could smelt his metal outside Pittsburgh, ship it to the East Coast and across the Atlantic to Birmingham and Sheffield, and undersell British-made steel in its home markets. The United States, which had been born in the country—at the first census fewer than 5 percent of the population lived in an urban environment—soon began to move to town. By 1900, as the following table shows, one-third of the population lived in cities, and three of ten urbanites lived in just five cities. But we should focus not only on the largest cities; the 85 urban places of 8,000 or more in 1850 had become 545 such places by 1900. Some of those places were what Gunther Barth has called "instant cities"—places like Denver, Salt Lake City, and Cheyenne—that popped up almost overnight. Others vaulted into urban status after decades of existence. For example, the hamlet in southwest Virginia that was Big Lick (pop. 400) in 1881 had become Roanoke (pop. 25,000) by 1892.

URBAN POPULATION, 1790–1900
(Cities of 8,000 or More)

Year	Population	% of Total Population	No. of Cities
1790	131,472	3.3	6
...			
1850	2.9 million	12.5	85
...			
1870	8 million	20.9	226
1880	11.3 million	22.6	286
1890	18.3 million	29.2	447
1900	25.0 million	33.1	545

Source: U.S. Census data

FIVE LARGEST CITIES, 1790–1900

Rank	1790		1850		1900	
1	New York	33,131	New York	515,000	New York	3.4 million
2	Philadelphia	28,552	Baltimore	169,000	Chicago	1.7 million
3	Boston	18,320	Boston	137,000	Philadelphia	1.3 million
4	Charleston	16,359	Philadelphia	121,000	St. Louis	575,000
5	Baltimore	13,503	New Orleans	116,000	Boston	560,000

Source: *U.S. Department of Commerce, Bureau of the Census,* Atlas of the Census, 1900 *(Washington, D.C., 1901)*

This rapid growth—another hallmark of the industrial revolutions—brought with it the economic dislocations about which Donnelly and others complained. Mass unemployment struck the cities, and a disastrous fall in commodity prices and land values impoverished many farmers. Wheat, which had sold for more than a dollar a bushel in the 1870s, fell below thirty cents in the second half of the 1890s, while the price of cotton, which had averaged better than ten cents a pound in the 1870s, dropped under seven cents during most of the 1890s. The average value of farmland per acre actually fell about 7 percent between 1890 and 1900, the first such decline in U.S. history.

In national politics these economic dislocations produced what historians have called the Populist revolt. By the end of the 1890s it helped to shatter the relative political equilibrium that had existed in the post–Civil War decades and produced what political scientists call the fourth American party system, an era of Republican hegemony which lasted until the Great Depression of the 1930s. But it must be remembered that the Populists, though their party made the last major challenge to the two-party system in America, never gained significant political power. For a real understanding of the politics of the 1890s, it is necessary to look at the major parties.

The Democrats, who regained the White House in the election of 1892, stood basically for "personal liberty, negative government, and local autonomy," as Robert Wesser has pointed out. Relatively speaking, the Republicans favored a more active government, but nothing that remotely resembled the kind of social service state that was developing in European nations such as Britain and Germany. The parties differed chiefly on tariff and pension policy. Most Republicans favored high tariffs and larger pensions for Union Army Civil War veterans; most Democrats favored low tariffs and smaller pensions. But most Gilded Age politicians shared similar values and would have agreed with the publicist John Fiske who argued that government existed "to protect the property of men and the honor of women." They favored not an activist government but what has been called the "nightwatchman state."

Grover Cleveland, elected president in 1884 and 1892, not only exemplified those values but his three races for the presidency illustrate nicely what we would now call the political gridlock of the twenty years after 1876. Examining the two-party popular vote—which Cleveland won each time, even though Benjamin Harrison received more electoral votes in 1888 and thus became president—we see that Cleveland won by 23,000 votes out of nearly 10 million in 1884, by 436 out of more than 11 million in 1888, and by a relatively comfortable 380,000 out of 12 million in 1892. But although each president between Grant's victory in 1872 and McKinley's in 1896 was a minority president, Cleveland's percentage of the popular vote in 1892—46.2 percent—was the smallest. The defeated incumbent president, Harrison, won only 43 percent. More than a million voters had voted for the Populist candidate, and another quarter-million for the Prohibitionist.

Perhaps the best single example of Cleveland's conservative policies in domestic affairs is his veto, on principle, of a bill passed by Congress to provide $50,000 of relief, in the form of seed, for farmers in a drought-stricken area. "The people," Cleveland's veto message ran, "ought to support the government, but the government ought not to support the people." In foreign affairs he opposed American expansion, refusing to approve either a recognition of Cuban rebels in their struggle against Spain or the annexation of Hawaii after American planters, with the help of the U.S. navy, had led a successful coup in 1893 against Queen Liliuokalani.

The depression of the 1890s broke the deadlock and created a demand for change. The election of 1896 is the first in two decades that cannot be written off as a choice between Tweedledum and Tweedledee. Insurgent Democrats repudiated the policies of Grover Cleveland and nominated William Jennings Bryan, who campaigned on many of the Populists' issues and won the nomination of their party as well. The Republicans nominated William McKinley, an Ohio politician who had been governor of his state and was best known as a high-tariff congressman. While many issues divided the candidates, the battle over a deliberately inflationary monetary policy, which would have brought relief to many overmortgaged farmers but done little positive for most Americans, became the focal point of the campaign. Bryan supported "free silver," a policy designed to be inflationary, while McKinley championed a presumably noninflationary gold standard.

The campaign set precedents for the coming century. Bryan, a spellbinding orator, crisscrossed the country, delivering speeches as no previous presidential candidate had. McKinley, a lackluster speaker, stayed home in Canton, Ohio, meeting on his front porch with carefully screened delegations of citizens. The innovations in his campaign were supplied by its manager, Marcus Alonzo Hanna, a wealthy Ohio manufacturer. Hanna raised unprecedented amounts of money, largely from what we now call "fat cats." These innovations—hectic campaigning and increasing dependence on rich contributors—would soon become standard for both national parties.

McKinley's election coincided with a cyclical upturn in the economy. As expected and promised, the new administration soon raised tariffs and in 1900 adopted the gold standard. In the long run the gold standard may have been more inflationary than a silver standard would have been, as new discoveries in Alaska and South Africa led to greater supplies of gold.

McKinley's victory, repeated even more decisively in 1900, began a period of Republican ascendancy: Woodrow Wilson in 1912 and 1916 was the only Democrat to win the White House between 1892 and 1932, and the first of his victories was made possible by a progressive/conservative split in the GOP. This Republican dominance was accompanied by decreasing voter participation, a weakening of party organizations, and the substitution of issues about industrial regulation and the welfare of labor for those of the money question and civil service reform. Although foreign policy had not been an issue in the 1896 campaign, McKinley's triumph over Bryan meant the adoption of what imperialists such as navy Captain Alfred Thayer Mahan called a "large policy." This view insisted that in order to achieve greatness the United States must have bases all over the maritime world at which its navy could obtain coal and other necessary supplies. Thus after the United States provoked Spain into war over Cuba in 1898—a war presumably fought for anti-imperialist ends ("Cuba Libre"/"Free Cuba" was a popular slogan)—the United States became an imperialist power. It established a protectorate over Cuba, annexed Puerto Rico in the Caribbean, and seized a chain of island bases across the Pacific Ocean and the Philippine Islands. This last acquisition made the United States a player in Asian politics, which placed it on a collision course with Japan, and, in the later twentieth century, led to three separate American wars in Asia. In the short run, however, the policy was popular, and when Bryan chose to fight the election of 1900 partly on opposition to Philippine annexation, the result was an even greater victory for the Republicans than in 1896.

This is the background which makes the ethnocultural history of the 1890s understandable.

As the century neared its end, Native Americans faced the continuing encroachment of other Americans into lands they considered theirs. Although neither the superintendent of the census nor Frederick Jackson Turner mentioned it, the year 1890 marked the last large-scale bloody clash between armed Indians and the United States Army. In the massacre at Wounded Knee, Dakota Territory, just after Christmas, soldiers killed some 250 men, women, and children, most of them unarmed. Many years later Black Elk, an Ogalala Sioux and a survivor of the massacre, remembered:

> I did not know then how much was ended. When I look back now from this high hill of my old age, I can still see the butchered women and children lying heaped and scattered all along the crooked gulch as plain as when I saw them with my eyes still young. And I can see that something else died there in that bloody mud, and was buried in the blizzard. A people's dream died there.

But what well-meaning white reformers, lawyers, and politicians now did with words and laws was even more devastating to Indian culture than what the army had done with

Gatling guns and sabers. Many believed that the Indian was
destined to disappear—it was traditional to speak of "the vanishing American"—and in fact the 1890 census showed Indian population down to 250,000. Since scholars now believe
that before the arrival of the white man there were several
million native Americans in what is now the United States,
this was a drastic reduction. One historian of Amerindians is
so impressed by the massive depopulation that he speaks of
the "widowed land."

Pressure for reform of the government's Indian policy had
been sparked by Helen Hunt Jackson's *A Century of Dishonor*
(1881), which told the discreditable story of the broken
promises and mistreatment the Indians had endured. Most
white reformers believed that traditional patterns of Indian
culture, particularly the practice of holding land in common,
were the greatest barriers to the Indian becoming "a good
white man," and therefore had to be destroyed if the Indian
people were to be saved. As one reformer put it: "Humanity
calls loudly for some interposition on the part of the American
government to save, if possible, some portion of these ill-fated
tribes; and this, it is thought, can only be done by furnishing
them the means, and generally turning their attention to agricultural pursuits."

Many in Congress agreed; others saw the reform movement
as an opportunity for some whites to gain possession of Indian
land, which government policy had long forbidden. This
combination of interests produced the so-called Dawes Act of
1887. It enabled individual Indians to obtain title to former
tribal lands—160 acres to families, 80 acres to individual
adults. After allocations to individuals had been made, many
of the remaining tribal lands were declared surplus and made
available for sale to non-Indians.

One contemporary critic of the Dawes Act, Republican

Senator Henry M. Teller of Colorado, argued in Congress that granting individual titles to Indians was in the interest of land-hungry whites and that "when thirty or forty years shall have passed and these Indians shall have parted with their [lands], they will curse the hand that was raised professedly in their defense. . . ." Historians have almost universally agreed with the senator and declared the Dawes Act a disaster. It failed to achieve the reformers' purposes: very few Indians were integrated into the broader society. It did meet the hopes of some unscrupulous whites, as it cost Indians about two-fifths of their land holdings. In 1887 the tribes had owned some 138 million acres; by 1900 the total acreage in Indian hands had fallen to some 78 million acres. This loss of land was one aspect of the dying dream to which Black Elk referred.

Well-meaning but destructive reformers attacked Indian culture in other ways. Many of the officials on the reservations were also Christian missionaries, and their policies usually favored Indians who had become Christians. The reformers did bring needed education to Indian peoples, but often did so in environments that were hostile to Indian culture. The government sponsored boarding schools in which Indian culture was banned and located them far from where most Indians lived.

In the American South other dreams were dying. Some Americans, black and white, had dreamed that the abolition of slavery at the end of the Civil War would usher in an era of racial democracy in the South, where more than 90 percent of the nation's nine million African Americans still lived in 1890. While the abandonment of that dream by most Northern politicians had been going on for some time, the "corrupt bargain" of 1877 makes a convenient demarcation line. That bargain settled the "stolen" presidential election of 1876, the only presidential election to be settled by Congress because of a dispute over who had actually been elected. Southern Democrats agreed, after months of wrangling, to the installation of Republican Rutherford B. Hayes as president in return for the withdrawal of federal troops who were required to maintain even the semblance of political democracy in the South. The last serious attempt of the Republican party to "reconstruct" the South came in 1890, when the so-called Force Bill, sponsored by Massachusetts Republican Congressman Henry Cabot Lodge, was hotly debated in Congress. Under its terms, if one hundred voters within a congressional district or a city of twenty thousand or more believed there had been fraud in an election, they could petition the federal circuit courts to appoint a board to determine the validity of the charges. Although specifically aimed at the South, which had already disfranchised many and perhaps most black voters, the bill would have applied anywhere and might well have been used to challenge machine voting in the urban North as well. But it was defeated. Massive disfranchisement of potential African-American voters in the South continued for seventy-five years until Lyndon B. Johnson's 1965 Voting Rights Act.

In addition to disfranchisement, Southern state governments during the late nineteenth and early twentieth centuries passed laws creating and "perfecting" the system of legal segregation known as Jim Crow. The "perfection" included applying the law to new inventions, for example telephone booths. In most Southern states other laws were enacted requiring voters to be able to "interpret" a clause of the state constitution. The right of undereducated whites to vote was supposed to be protected by "grandfather clauses," which exempted from the requirement anyone whose grandfather had voted. But large numbers of Southern white voters were disfranchised, along with almost all blacks, largely by the poll tax, a tax that had to be paid only if one wished to vote. In the 1880s more than two-thirds of Southern white men had voted, but by the early twentieth century fewer than one in three did; in some deep South states the turnout was less than 15 percent. The Southern version of the Populist revolt represented an unsuccessful attempt by some poor white Southern farmers and their spokesmen to overturn the existing political system, an attempt that was in large part wrecked by the failure of poor whites and blacks to unite.

Most Southern blacks and their leaders, of whom the former slave Booker T. Washington is the outstanding example, felt they were forced to accommodate to segregation. In his famous—some would say infamous—"Atlanta Compromise" speech in 1893, Washington, speaking to a mixed but segregated audience, offered the white South a bargain: "In all things that are purely social [the races] can be as separate as the fingers, yet one as the hand in all things essential to mutual progress." The bargain, of course, was not accepted. Although apologists for the white South spoke of "separate but equal" societies and facilities, nothing even resembling equal facilities for blacks existed.

Another African-American leader, Massachusetts-born W. E. B. Du Bois, a Harvard-trained Ph.D. in history, is usually thought of as an ideological antagonist of Booker T. Washington. But it is too often forgotten that Du Bois too could celebrate African-American accommodation within the Jim Crow system. Writing of Atlanta around the turn of the century, Du Bois noted that a black man

> may rise in the morning in a house which a black man built and which he himself owns, it has been painted and papered by black men; the furniture was probably bought at a white store, but not necessarily, and if it was it was brought to the house by a colored drayman. He starts to work walk-

ing to the car with a colored neighbor and sitting in a part of the car surrounded by colored people; in most cases he works for white men but not in all [and even if his employer was white his fellow workmen were black]. Once a week he reads a colored paper; he is insured in a colored insurance company; he patronizes a colored school with colored teachers, and a colored church with a colored preacher; he gets his amusements at places frequented and usually run by colored people; he is buried by a colored undertaker in a colored graveyard.

But even in this New South Atlanta, as Du Bois well knew, most black men and women were desperately poor and owned very little.

Although there were no national Jim Crow laws, the federal government in many ways countenanced their application. For example, it sanctioned segregation throughout the nation's capital, just as it had earlier permitted slave auctions there. The so-called Second Morrill Act of 1890 permitted states to divide federal funds in support of agricultural and mechanical arts colleges between separate institutions for white and black students. No president between Grant, who left office in 1877, and Truman, who became president in 1945, paid much attention to the civil rights of African Americans, and after 1890 the same was true of almost all those in the legislative branch of government. But it was the judicial branch that placed the ultimate stamp of approval on Jim Crow.

In the *Civil Rights Cases* of 1883 the Supreme Court had ruled in five separate cases that discriminating against African-American citizens in public places by private means was constitutional. The Court thus negated the thrust of the Civil Rights Act of 1875, one of the key pieces of Reconstruction legislation. The preamble of the 1875 act had laid down strong egalitarian principles—"we recognize the equality of all men before the law and hold that it is the duty of government . . . to mete out equal and exact justice to all of whatever nativity, race, color, or persuasion, religious or political"—that sound quite modern except for the omission of women.

Only Justice Harlan supported those principles. A Kentuckian and a former slaveholder, he filed a lone dissent, insisting that racial discrimination was a "badge and incident" of slavery and thus prohibited under the "equal protection of the laws" clause of the Fourteenth Amendment. He directly contradicted the majority view, put forth by Joseph Bradley, which argued that "mere discriminations on account of race or color [are] not regarded as badges of slavery." Earlier, sounding like many contemporary opponents of affirmative action, Bradley insisted that "When a man has emerged from slavery, and by the aid of beneficent legislation has shaken off the inseparable concomitants of that state, there must be some stage in the progress of his elevation when he takes the rank of a mere citizen, and ceases to be the special favorite of the laws, and when his rights are to be protected in the ordinary modes by which other men's rights are protected."

In 1883 the Court was willing to permit discrimination only in public places when it was done by private parties, holding that such discrimination was constitutional. Given his green light, Southern states went a step farther and began enacting the Jim Crow laws that enforced racial segregation by statute and ordinance. Thirteen years later a case challenging statutory discrimination came before the Court.

In 1896, by a vote of 8 to 1 in the landmark case of *Plessy v. Ferguson*, the Supreme Court ruled that governments could enforce segregation by statute. *Plessy* was not, as is often assumed, about school segregation. The case concerned the segregation of interstate railroad passengers. The plaintiff,

Homer A. Plessy, about whom very little is known, was a well-to-do citizen of New Orleans of mixed racial ancestry, what was then called a mulatto. He wished to travel in a Pullman car, which he could afford, but was denied the right to purchase such a ticket because of his race. (He was told that if he wished to purchase enough tickets for an entire Pullman car, he could ride in it.) Plessy went to court. In his original suit he did not challenge segregation itself but argued that since he had more white than black ancestry, the law should not apply to him. He lost the case and only then proceeded to challenge segregation itself on constitutional grounds.

Justice Henry B. Brown of Michigan spoke for himself and seven other Supreme Court justices:

> We consider the underlying fallacy of the plaintiff's argument to consist in the assumption that the enforced separation of the two races stamps the colored race with a badge of inferiority. If this be so, it is not by reason of anything found in the act, but solely because the colored race chooses to put that construction upon it.

The decision went on to sanction, by extension, various kinds of government-enforced segregation as long as what became known as "separate but equal accommodations" were provided. In a closing paragraph which had little to do with law, Justice Brown made these observations:

> Legislation is powerless to eradicate racial instincts or to abolish distinctions based upon physical differences, and the attempt to do so can only result in accentuating the difficulties of the present situation. If the civil and political rights of both races be equal, one cannot be inferior to the other civilly or politically. If one race be inferior to the other socially, the Constitution of the United States cannot put them on the same plane.

Again Harlan was the sole dissenter, insisting that the "separate but equal" proviso was a sham and predicting, quite accurately, that separate accommodations would never be equal.

> The thin disguise of "equal" accommodations for passengers in railroad coaches will not mislead anyone, or atone for the wrong this day done.... The statute of Louisiana is inconsistent with the personal liberty of citizens, black and white ... and hostile to both the spirit and letter of the Constitution.... If laws of like character should be enacted in the several states of the Union, the effect would be in the highest degree mischievous. Slavery as an institution tolerated by law would, it is true, have disappeared ... there would remain a power in the states by sinister legislation, to interfere with the full enjoyment of the blessings of freedom; to regulate civil rights, common to all citizens, upon the basis of race; and to place in a condition of legal inferiority a large body of American citizens....

African Americans in the 1890s were thus abandoned by all three branches of the federal government and largely left to the tender mercies of oligarchic white Southern state governments. No wonder the historian Rayford W. Logan described the era as the "nadir" of black American life, even though, as Justice Harlan noted, slavery had disappeared.

An examination of late-nineteenth-century socioeconomic data underlines the inferior conditions of life that African Americans had to endure. Their income was significantly less than that of their white neighbors, their life expectancy years shorter, and their infant and maternal mortality rates much higher than those of whites. Lynchings and other forms of terrorism were a constant threat. In the 1880s a few more whites were lynched than blacks, but in the 1890s and after lynchings were perpetrated largely against blacks. More than a thousand black Americans were lynched in the 1890s; in no year before

1917 did the toll fall below fifty. What is to be wondered at is the amount of social progress African Americans were able to achieve. In the first post–Civil War census (1870), 79 percent of African Americans over ten years of age were recorded as illiterate; thirty years later the census of 1900 reported a figure of just under 45 percent. (The comparable figures for whites were just under 12 percent and just over 6 percent.)

The situation of immigrant Americans was much more diverse than that of either Native Americans or African Americans. In the first place they were more numerous. In every census between 1860 and 1920, about one American in seven was listed as foreign-born; if one counts their American-born children, the second generation, the figure becomes one in three. In the second place their origins and circumstances were much more varied.

Despite these variations, which will be examined below, all immigrants in the 1890s shared certain experiences and problems—except for the excluded Chinese, whose situation was, in many ways, unique. By the 1890s immigrants benefited from the growth of industry, which employed most workers; they suffered from the depression that wracked much of the decade. In common with all migrants, they had problems of adjustment and acculturation.

In the wake of the Chinese exclusion, many immigrants experienced threats to their entrance to the United States. All felt, to some degree, the first touches of federal regulation. In 1882, the very year of Chinese exclusion, Congress also began general immigration restriction. It authorized the exclusion of "any convict, lunatic, idiot, or any person unable to take care of himself or herself without becoming a public charge." It also enacted a small head tax (fifty cents) on each immigrant entering by sea to defray the expenses of immigration accommodation and inspection. (Nothing better highlights the differences between immigration concerns in the Gilded Age and those of today than to note that when, in 1894, it was pointed out that seaborne passengers from both Canada and Mexico were taxed but those coming overland were not, Congress exempted immigrants coming by sea from Mexico and Canada from the tax!)

Changes in American immigration laws were largely dictated by a growing conviction that the nature of immigration was changing and that the nation's unlimited opportunities were closing. In addition to these long-term factors, the depression of the 1890s raised fears about unfair immigrant competition for jobs. By the 1890s Americans were acutely aware of the vast increase in the volume of immigration and of distinct changes in its ethnic composition. More than five million immigrants had come in the 1880s, almost twice as many as in any previous decade. And although about two-thirds of those were from familiar regions of western Europe, more than one in six came from southern or eastern Europe and seemed particularly alien to many Americans.

While on the West Coast it was the Chinese who were the prime target of nativists, in late-nineteenth-century New England it was French Canadians who came under attack. Between 1870 and 1900 a third colonization of New England (the English constituted the first and the Irish the second) brought more than half a million French Canadians to mill towns chiefly in Massachusetts and Rhode Island. In 1881, just as Congress was passing anti-Chinese legislation, a respected public official unleashed a tirade against these immigrants, likening them to the Chinese. According to Carroll D. Wright, Massachusetts' commissioner of labor statistics and a noted reformer:

> The Canadian French are the Chinese of the Eastern
> States. They care nothing for our institutions. . . . They do
> not come to make a home among us . . . their purpose is
> merely to sojourn a few years as aliens . . . and, when they
> have gathered out of us what will satisfy their ends, to get
> them from whence they came, and bestow it there. They
> are a horde of industrial invaders, not a stream of stable set-
> tlers.

While many French Canadians did go back and forth—as
did millions of immigrants of other nationalities—large numbers formed stable American communities. By 1900 the census
found more than 800,000 French Canadians of the first and
second generations. We can get a somewhat idealized picture
of French Canadian immigrant life from the novel *Jeanne la
Fileuse* (Jeanne the Mill Girl), published in Massachusetts in
1878 by an immigrant journalist, Honoré Beaugrand. Jeanne
and her family leave Montreal by train at 4 p.m. one day and
arrive in Fall River at 2 p.m. the next. They pay $10 apiece for
their tickets, and the railroad and the mill owners make the
journey simple: although they must change trains twice, bilin-
gual personnel are on hand to show them the way, and their
baggage is delivered to the flat the mill has provided.

The French Canadians were the only ethnic group whose
chief means of immigration was the train, and, unlike most
late-nineteenth-century immigrants, they moved as complete
families. Yet in other ways their experience was similar to that
of many other migrant ethnic groups. By the mid-1870s some
95 percent of transatlantic immigrant passengers came by
steamship rather than sail, and by the 1880s most came on
ships specially constructed for the immigrant trade, which had
become a modern big business. The Atlantic immigrant trade
was dominated by a few European lines—no American company had a significant share—among which the British Cu-

nard and the German North German Lloyd and Hamburg
Amerika (HAPAG) lines were preeminent. Modern
steamships meant shorter crossing times (days instead of
weeks), improved (though not necessarily good) shipboard
conditions, and, because of the keen competition, lower fares.

The major lines sold tickets on both sides of the Atlantic.
By the 1890s HAPAG, for example, had perhaps three thousand agents in the United States, most of whom were ethnic
entrepreneurs who sold tickets as a sideline. By the turn of the
century perhaps every third immigrant came on prepaid tickets. These were purchased in the New World for some specific
immigrant in the Old, and were often combined with railroad
tickets at either or both ends. Thus an immigrant in Detroit
who wished to help a relative or friend come over from
Poland could buy a combination ticket from a HAPAG agent.
The ticket could be picked up from a HAPAG agent in
Krakow. The company would provide the immigrant with
rail transportation from Krakow to Hamburg, room and
board in Hamburg until the ship was ready for boarding,
steerage passage to New York, and a railroad ticket from New
York to Detroit. After 1892 such an immigrant would be
quickly processed at Ellis Island and ferried to either Manhattan or Hoboken to catch the appropriate train.

Like their predecessors, late-nineteenth-century immigrants came to the United States for work, work that was increasingly urban and industrial. While some European
workers, like many French Canadians, were recruited by employers (museums in Cornwall, England, for example, still
preserve handbills and posters proclaiming the presence of
"good paying jobs" in various American mining districts),
perhaps the majority were participating in what we now call
chain migration. In that kind of migration, immigrants follow
one another, not just from Europe to America but to a particu-

lar place in America where an earlier immigrant—a relative, a neighbor, or, as some Europeans would say, a *landsman*, a *paisano*—was already established. The established immigrant might even have a job waiting for the newcomer: referral hiring was more common than direct recruiting. An American consul in Naples reported in 1890 a typical explanation for emigrating he heard there: "My friend in America is doing well and he has sent for me." Similar migration chains moved many immigrant workers around the United States.

Migration chains, which exist in almost all migration, help to account for the most characteristic social phenomenon of immigrant America, the ethnic neighborhood or enclave. In recent years it has become trendy to speak of these as "ghettos," but the term is inappropriate. True ghettos are enforced by the larger society; America's ethnic neighborhoods were created by the immigrants themselves. Thus while leaving home was certainly an "uprooting," many if not most immigrants in this era moved into neighborhoods with some familiar characteristics, for they were filled with kith and kin and contained transplanted institutions, including ethnic churches and secular organizations.

Although these neighborhoods nurtured the immigrants, they also provided ammunition for detractors. The arguments used against the Chinese, the French Canadians, and other immigrant groups usually included the charge that they were clannish, kept to themselves, and did not really care for their new country. These were not new charges; they were older than the United States. In the 1750s Benjamin Franklin, among others, had attacked the Germans in Pennsylvania on just such grounds, pretending to believe that the German language would drive out English in Pennsylvania.

Nativist or anti-immigrant movements have risen periodically in American history. The most notorious was the Know

Nothing movement of the 1840s and 1850s; its chief targets were Catholic immigrants, mostly Irish and German, who seemed to the typical Protestant Know Nothing to threaten the Republic. Although the Know Nothings made great political strides and elected many congressmen and state officials, they were never able to achieve the restriction of immigration and the tightening of naturalization laws. In the 1890s a second national anti-Catholic organization, the American Protective Association, gained a short-lived prominence, but by that time anti-Catholicism alone could not sustain national political goals.

The most significant and effective anti-immigrant organization in the 1890s was the Immigration Restriction League, founded in 1894 by a group of Harvard graduates. The League's leaders, caught up in what its historian has called "the Anglo-Saxon complex," campaigned relentlessly for an immigration policy based on ethnocultural discrimination. Its founder, Prescott F. Hall, argued that the American people had to decide whether they wanted their country "to be peopled by British, German and Scandinavian stock, historically free, energetic, progressive, or by Slav, Latin and Asiatic races [this latter referred to Jews rather than Chinese or Japanese], historically down-trodden, atavistic and stagnant."

The League and its chief political spokesman, Henry Cabot Lodge, the scholar in politics who represented Massachusetts in Congress from 1887 to 1924, eventually settled on a literacy test as the best means to bring about a general restriction of immigration. The House passed a literacy bill five times—in 1895, 1897, 1913, 1915, and 1917—and was joined by the Senate on all but the first occasion. Each bill that passed was vetoed by presidents as diverse as Grover Cleveland, William Howard Taft, and Woodrow Wilson; the final veto was overridden in 1917.

Cleveland's veto message denounced the literacy test as "a radical departure" and argued that the nation's "stupendous growth" had been "largely due to the assimilation and thrift of millions of sturdy and patriotic adopted citizens." He reminded the nation that some "immigrants who, with their descendants, are now numbered among our best citizens" were once attacked as undesirable, and characterized the bill as "illiberal, narrow and un-American." The literacy test did not impress him: "It is infinitely more safe to admit a hundred thousand immigrants who, although unable to read and write, seek among us only a home and an opportunity to work than to admit one of those unruly agitators and enemies of governmental control who can not only read and write, but delights in arousing by inflammatory speech the illiterate and peacefully inclined to discontent and tumult."

The timing of the nativists' successes in Congress is instructive. In 1895 and 1897 the severe economic depression was surely a major factor; the return of prosperity deprived nativists of a congressional majority for almost two decades. The elite leaders of the League were able to win support from broad areas of the politically active population, particularly from the leaders of organized labor, most of whom saw the plentiful supply of immigrant labor as an impediment to their ability to organize and improve the conditions of American workers. As Samuel Gompers, the British-born leader of the American Federation of Labor put it, in an analogy to the protective tariff which was standard American political economy, a country that kept out "pauper made goods" should also keep out the pauper. Conversely, most employers wanted continuation of unrestricted numbers of potential workers.

In 1891 Congress and President Benjamin Harrison responded to anti-immigrant pressure groups by passing additional restrictions on free, white immigrants, by barring entrance to "All idiots, insane persons, paupers or persons likely to become a public charge, persons suffering from a loathsome or a dangerous contagious disease, persons who have been convicted of a felony or other infamous crime or misdemeanor involving moral turpitude, polygamists. . . ."

For the first time the 1891 act made events that occurred after immigration grounds for expulsion: anyone who became a public charge "within one year after his arrival" was deemed to have entered in violation of the law.

The restriction against polygamists was aimed at Mormons, not Muslims, and was largely chimerical. Earlier in the century Mormons had recruited successfully in Europe, particularly in England and Scandinavia, and had assisted the immigration of tens of thousands of their converts. But by 1891 the Mormon Perpetual Immigration Fund had been confiscated by the U.S. government, and a revelation had caused the Mormon church to disavow polygamy.

These new restrictions were largely symbolic, at least in the 1890s. Between 1892 and 1900 only 22,515 potential immigrants were excluded, a mere seven-tenths of 1 percent of the total. As noted earlier, by 1892 the federal immigration station on Ellis Island was in operation, and the newly created federal immigration bureaucracy had begun to grow.

Immigration and the attitudes about it were clearly in flux in the 1890s, changing as the country and its needs changed. The notion of a closed frontier, however ambiguous that may seem to us today, was a powerful influence on contemporary minds, persuading many that growth and opportunity would be more limited in a frontierless society. Those of little faith thus believed in limiting immigration. Not surprisingly, Frederick Jackson Turner spent much of his last unproductive years at the Huntington Library musing about the evils of unrestricted immigration. The seeds of the immigration restriction of the 1920s were surely planted in the 1880s and 1890s, but that the mature plants bore the bitter fruit they did was largely due to developments in the twentieth century.

However gloomy much of the 1890s had been, for most Americans the century ended on a dual note of triumph. Domestically the economy turned upward sometime in 1896–1897; by 1898 the journalist Ray Stannard Baker could write that "every barn in Kansas has a fresh coat of paint," denoting the return of prosperity to a former hotbed of populism. The results of the Spanish-American War pleased most Americans, so that the election and reelection of William McKinley in 1896 and 1900 were an expression of confidence in things as they were. Although America's colonial mission was imbued with racism, neither race nor ethnicity figured significantly in those campaigns; Bryan, the less conservative candidate, also represented some of the most racist elements in American society. Native Americans and African Americans were increasingly ignored by most other Americans, the one largely isolated on desolate reservations, the other still chiefly resident in the South. Immigrants, however, dominating the cores of American cities, had become and would remain a central concern to the American body politic.

2

The Limits of Progressivism

HISTORIANS have called the years from the turn of the century to the entry of the United States into World War I in 1917 the Progressive Era. For a time the traditional interpretation treated progressivism as a great crusade involving most of the nation. But analyses of the movement by George E. Mowry and Alfred D. Chandler demonstrated that progressivism was not only led by a relatively narrow middle-class professional elite, but, as Mowry noted perceptively, that it was, for all intents and purposes, a progressivism for old American stock whites only. While some progressive leaders, such as Theodore Roosevelt, at least paid lip service to ethnic democracy, others, such as Woodrow Wilson, were openly and blatantly racist, and contemptuous of most recent immigrants. Wilson did change his tune about immigrants—but not about African Americans—when he had to compete for ethnic votes in 1912 and 1916.

To be sure, the great issues in the Progressive Era did not center on race and ethnicity. Concerned and often alarmed by the growth of industry and large cities, progressive reformers sought to create a society that could fulfill what one of them called "the promise of American life." To that end progressives strove for changes in the forms of government, passing constitutional amendments that made the Senate directly responsible to the electorate. With less enthusiasm they extended suffrage to women and in many localities sponsored such governmental reforms as the secret ballot, the direct primary, recall, initiative, and referendum. But this seeming bow to the popular will was balanced by enhancing the powers of "experts." Progressives advocated city managers and the commission form of government, and increasingly tried to place matters into the hands of regulatory and investigative commissions largely independent of the political process. All of this was capped in 1919 by the "noble experiment" of Prohibition, one of the most dismal failures in the history of American reform. If historians are no longer as enthusiastic about the progressive "age of reform" as they once were—after all, there is now the New Deal and the Great Society to consider, when reform made much more substantial changes in the American way of life—they nevertheless tend to be generous in appraising its achievements and tolerant of its failings.

Seen from the point of view of racial and ethnic minorities, the period could very well be called the "regressive era," a time in which things grew a little worse, a time when nativism and racism gained strength and acceptance at all levels of society. American Indians, African Americans, and immigrants could each point to particular repressive measures, acts, and, above all, attitudes which made it clear that the promises of American life were not meant for them. These activities and attitudes are the concern here, and not the various phases of progressive reform—such as "trust busting"—that are most often the focus of historians' attention.

The American Indian, as Donald Parman has noted, "was primarily a bystander, seldom a participant, often a victim, and rarely a beneficiary of the progressive reforms." As western states were added to the Union—Oklahoma (1907), Arizona and New Mexico (1912)—generally unsympathetic white Westerners gained more and more influence over Indian affairs. Nothing better symbolizes progressive indifference to the concerns of Indians than Theodore Roosevelt's response to Chief No Shirt, when the Indian leader came to the nation's capital to complain about government mistreatment. Since the visit had not been authorized by the Bureau of Indian Affairs (BIA), Roosevelt refused to see him. After No Shirt had returned to his reservation, the president wrote him an admonitory note, dripping with self-righteous rectitude and stressing the hyperassimilationist philosophy that characterized the progressive approach to the "lesser breeds without the law":

> ... The earth is occupied by the white people and the red people. ... If the red people would prosper, they must follow the mode of life which has made the white people so strong; and that it is only right that the white people should show the red people what to do and how to live right. ... I wish to be a father to the red people as to the white. ... Now my friend ... Try to set your people a good example of upright and industrious life, patience under difficulties, and respect for the authority of the officers I have appointed. ... If you try as hard to help them as you do to find something in their conduct to censure, you will be surprised to find how much satisfaction life holds in store for you.

On the crucial question of Indian lands, Roosevelt's administration not only continued many of the policies that had shifted millions of Indian acres into white hands but also, in the name of conservation, tried to wrest timberlands worth millions of dollars from the control of Indian tribes. In the closing days of the Roosevelt presidency, TR and his chief forester, Gifford Pinchot, concocted executive orders transferring to the Forest Service fifteen million acres of timberlands from several Indian reservations that had been created or expanded by earlier executive orders. Even more potentially damaging than the loss of those lands was the theory that Roosevelt enunciated: that Indians had no rights to those reservation lands that had been granted by executive orders, and that the president could redispose of them at will. The BIA, which often tried to protect Indian property rights, opposed this interpretation, and it was reversed in the more legalistic Taft administration. The seized acres were returned to Indian control. Roosevelt and Pinchot may have been encouraged to take their imperious actions by the decision in *Lone Wolf v. Hitchcock* (1903), in which a unanimous Supreme Court held not only that Congress could unilaterally break Indian treaties but also that Indian lands could be seized by Congress without the consent of the tribes or compensation of any kind. As shocking as the *Lone Wolf* decision seems today, it was consistent with the nationalism of the post–Spanish-American War era—and, after all, it was handed down by a court similar in composition to the one that had affirmed segregation in *Plessy*.

The drive to assimilate the Indians, to make them as much as possible carbon copies of whites, at least in their way of life, was marked by dozens of inconsistencies. The most glaring of these was the mistreatment of the most assimilated large group of Indians in the country, the Five Civilized Tribes of eastern Oklahoma, the Cherokees, Chickasaws, Choctaws, Creeks, and Seminoles. Their history is a long and sad one. Most of them were descended from more than 100,000 Indians who had been exiled from the Southeast by President Andrew Jackson and forced to march to Oklahoma in the 1830s along what they came to call the Trail of Tears. Those who survived were established in Indian Territory—most of present-day Oklahoma—where they were to be "permanently" free of white encroachment and live under their own tribal governments and laws.

Like most agreements with Indians, those stating that Oklahoma was to be theirs alone were soon broken by whites. By 1890 Indians were only a sizable minority of the population: the census that year showed a little more than 100,000 whites, just over 50,000 Indians, and nearly 20,000 blacks in what was still officially Indian Territory. Politicians were already planning to make it a state. The Indian minority owned about half of present-day Oklahoma and more than half of the best and most valuable agricultural land, much of which was rich in oil, natural gas, and other minerals. The commission set up by the Dawes Act of 1893 had tried to dispossess the tribal governments and enforce "severalty"—that is, forcing the tribes to allow individuals to own specific parcels of land as opposed to communal ownership by the tribe—but had succeeded only in the case of the Seminoles. The Curtis Act of 1898 mandated the dissolution of tribal governments by 1906, and each of the tribes was eventually forced to accept an "agreement." This process was marked by fraud, bloodshed, and even murder, and resulted in what one scholar calls "the most important instance of Indian land loss in the twentieth century." Particularly shocking is that the chief perpetrators of the fraud and chicanery were some of the "best citizens" of Oklahoma, including public officials and Indian leaders. For example, the mestizo Cherokee leader, Robert Owen, later a U.S. senator, manipulated things so that he gained title to some ten thousand acres. But most of the illegal and unethical conduct benefited whites, not Indians or part-Indians. (Those interested in the details should read the classic account by Angie Debo, *And Still the Waters Run: The Betrayal of the Five*

Civilized Tribes.) The federal government made some attempts to protect the rights of Indians—efforts that were
often frustrated by local juries and judges—and a few whites
were beginning to organize pressure groups to protect Indians, such as the Indian Rights Association, which had been established in 1882. But most politicians and the people saw the
admission of Oklahoma to the Union in 1907 not as a product
of broken promises but as one more triumph of American civilization.

For African Americans the Progressive Era held promise—
that went unfulfilled. As the century began, Republican Representative George White of North Carolina, the last of a line
of Southern black congressmen that had begun during Reconstruction, made his valedictory speech before leaving Congress. Surveying the condition of black America, he insisted
that the American Negro

> asks no special favors, but simply demands that he be given
> the same chance for existence, for earning a livelihood, for
> raising himself in the scales of mankind and womanhood
> that are accorded to kindred nationalities.... Obliterate
> race hatred, party prejudice, and help us to achieve nobler
> ends, greater results, and become more satisfactory citizens
> to our brothers in white.
>
> This ... is perhaps the negro's temporary farewell to the
> American Congress; but let me say, Phoenix-like he will
> rise up some day and come again. These parting words are
> in behalf of an outraged, heart-broken, bruised, and bleed-
> ing, but God-fearing people, faithful, industrious, loyal
> people—rising people, full of potential force.

Later in 1901, newly installed President Theodore Roosevelt invited the black leader Booker T. Washington to have

dinner with him in the White House. This simple act of courtesy (when he remembered it, Roosevelt was a gentleman) created a furor and much harsh criticism of the president in the South, and won him little praise in the North. Roosevelt publicly insisted on his right to show hospitality to anyone, but he never again chose to invite an African American for a White House meal. More important, he and other Republican leaders embarked on a policy of "whitening" the Republican party in the South, a policy that would, later in the century, turn the party of Lincoln, Charles Sumner, and Thaddeus Stevens into a bastion of segregation.

Race relations in the Progressive Era were punctuated by numerous race riots, including affrays in New York City (1900), Springfield, Ohio (1904), Greensburg, Illinois (1906), Atlanta (1906), and Springfield, Illinois (1908). Unlike the riots of black rage that have become so common since the mid-sixties, and whose underlying causes are the abominable conditions in which the black urban underclass lives, the race riots of the early decades of the twentieth century were characterized by white mobs invading black neighborhoods, often in response to some offense, real or imagined, by an individual African American, offenses that ranged from rape and murder to mere "uppityness."

The riot in Atlanta on September 22, 1906, which showed how little different the New South was from the Old, was also one of the first—if not the first—riot in which a black American community was able to defend itself with some success. One contemporary account, by an anonymous African-American resident of Atlanta, spoke of

> The most horrible exhibition of savagery . . . in the treatment of negro passengers on the street cars as . . . they came into the public square—negro men, women and children

were beaten unmercifully. Even the negro barbers were dragged out of their shops while they were shaving white men, beaten and their shops demolished.

While there is no definitive account of the casualties, there seem to have been twenty-six persons killed—twenty-five blacks and one white—and a much larger number of persons of both races injured.

The riot in Springfield, Illinois, on August 14–15, 1908, was one of the earliest such riots outside the South in the twentieth century. Springfield was home to about 4,500 African Americans in a total population of some 60,000. The riot's triggering events were typical of the era: a murder and a rape allegedly committed by black men. According to the white reformer William English Walling, one of the mob's rallying cries was "Lincoln freed you, we'll show you where you belong." After the riot, in which 2 black men were lynched by the mob, 5 white men were killed by white rioters, 100 persons of both races but mainly blacks were seriously injured, 40 homes of Negroes were destroyed, and 2,000 of the city's African-American population were driven away, the leading local paper, the *Illinois State Journal*, could print the following, a classic example of what is called "blaming the victim":

> While all good citizens deplore the consequences of this outburst of the mob spirit... [it is] clear that conditions, not the populace, were to blame and that many good citizens could find no other remedy than that applied by the mob. It was not the fact of the whites' hatred toward the negroes, but the negroes' own misconduct, general inferiority or unfitness for free institutions that were at fault.

Such an event in Springfield, a city associated with Abraham Lincoln, shocked some Americans and led to the formation in 1909 of the National Association for the Advancement of Colored People (NAACP). Like the Indian Rights Association, the NAACP was established largely by white reformers, including Walling. W. E. B. Du Bois was the most prominent African American among its initial leaders. Four years earlier Du Bois, with twenty-eight other black intellectuals, had organized his first civil rights organization, the Niagara Movement, which is usually seen as the precursor to the NAACP and had similar goals. But the Niagara Movement was all black and the NAACP was integrated, mostly at the top. The NAACP evolved to become the major protest organization of African Americans and the first mass civil rights organization in American history. Its founders were unwilling to make the compromises with segregation that were accepted in Booker T. Washington's "Atlanta Compromise." Instead, from its very beginning, the NAACP pledged itself to work to abolish all forced segregation, to insist on education for black children equal to that given to white, and to work for the enforcement of the Fourteenth and Fifteenth Amendments, which mandated equal suffrage for blacks and prescribed political penalties—loss of representation—for states that limited the franchise rights of blacks, penalties which were never enforced. An essentially middle-class organization, the NAACP was largely silent on the economic grievances of black Americans.

From the first the NAACP's emphasis was on legal action. Its strategy of attacking state laws in the federal courts led to an impressive chain of victories all the way to *Brown v. Board of Education* (1954) and beyond. The first of these came in *Guinn v. U.S.* (1915). In that case the Supreme Court struck down the "grandfather clause" of the Oklahoma constitution which enabled illiterate whites to vote while denying that right to illiterate blacks. It won another important victory in *Buchanan v. Wiley* (1917) when the Supreme Court disallowed city ordinances requiring blacks and whites to live in separate blocks. This kind of legal urban segregation was relatively new: the first city ordinance requiring such separation had been adopted by Baltimore only in 1910.

But the Court's decisions often had little positive effect: Southern communities found ways to keep blacks from voting, and cities, particularly Northern cities, were able to create an increasingly effective system of residential segregation through the use of zoning laws, restrictive covenants, and the informal activities of real estate agents and homeowners' associations. Once residential segregation patterns had been established in Northern cities, it was usually relatively simple to locate public schools in places where all, or almost all, the pupils would be of one race. Beginning in the early years of this century, more and more Northern cities established segregated school systems in this manner, even though there were no Jim Crow laws on the statute books.

This segregation arose because of the slow but continuing migration of African Americans to cities. To be sure, nine of ten blacks still lived in the South. Between 1880 and 1900 the center of black population actually moved slightly south and west, from Walker County, Georgia, to De Kalb County, Alabama. While this population was still heavily rural, the 1900 census listed seventy-two cities, mostly in the South, with black populations of five thousand or more, while six of them—Philadelphia, New York, Baltimore, Washington, Memphis, and New Orleans—had more than fifty thousand. This urban migration, which continued for most of the twentieth century, was, like most migrations, primarily economic in its motivation. Politically it gained little in this era. While African Americans in Northern cities could exercise the right to vote, they had little or no political "clout." Although a number of Southern cities—including Charleston, Savannah,

Jacksonville, Montgomery, Shreveport, Baton Rouge, and Vicksburg—had Negro majorities, as did the entire state of Mississippi, the "sacred" American principle of majority rule was ignored in these places. No black person held elective political office in the South, and few were able to vote regardless of their educational qualifications.

The minority of blacks who lived in cities did enjoy better educational opportunities than those in rural areas, and there was something liberating in being free of the oppressive control of the plantation owner and small-town oligarchs. Yet economic opportunity was distinctly limited, both by employers and by labor unions. Most unions barred Negroes from membership so that, for example, skilled black artisans in the building trades found themselves excluded from the growing number of union-controlled jobs. This meant that black workers, even more than newly arrived immigrants, were ideal candidates for those who recruited strikebreakers in labor disputes.

One niche that black workers began to find for themselves was employment in the federal government. Since the Civil War it had been policy for Republican administrations to name a few prominent black men to relatively minor appointive positions—Frederick Douglass, for example, had been federal marshal for the District of Columbia and minister to Haiti. The rise of a federal civil service with its competitive exams meant that educated blacks could at least compete on equal terms for jobs at the lower rungs of the federal service. More than a few received Post Office jobs for which they were "overqualified." Thus when the Wilson administration began instituting segregation in the federal service in 1913, it came as a shock.

The change in policy was instituted by Wilson's postmaster general, a Texan who claimed to be startled to discover that in the railway mail service, black and white postal employees, all male, shared toilet facilities. It was soon decreed that Post Office workers must use separate toilets; since in the crowded rail cars in which postal workers sorted mail there was room for only one toilet, black workers lost those jobs. The Virginia-born Wilson upheld his subordinate. Wilson himself contributed to rising levels of Northern antiblack prejudice by publicly endorsing the racist motion picture *The Birth of a Nation* (1915), which glorified the Ku Klux Klan and demeaned blacks as rapists and cowardly simpletons. "History written with lightning," the onetime history professor called it.

If the events of Indian and African-American history in the early years of the century could scarcely be called encouraging, the history of immigrants and immigrant groups is much more varied. The first fourteen years of the century represent the peak years of immigration to the United States: some thirteen million immigrants had entered from 1901 to 1914, when the outbreak of World War I interrupted most immigration streams from Europe. During that period the annual incidence of immigration to the United States was higher than it has been before or since: each year more than ten immigrants arrived for each thousand persons already in the United States, nearly twice the rate that had prevailed in the 1890s. Yet because many immigrants returned home, and because total population was growing steadily, the percentage of foreign-born persons in the United States did not change materially, as the following table shows.

More and more Americans nonetheless became convinced that immigration was a serious problem, not only because of the increasing numbers of immigrants but because of what they saw as the changing nature of the flow. And it was not only the zealots of the Immigration Restriction League or the traditionally anti-immigrant trade union leaders who were concerned about immigration. Many middle-class Americans, including reformers who saw the "Americanization" of immigrants as one of their major tasks, came to feel that the sheer size of immigration had to be reduced.

FOREIGN-BORN AS A PERCENTAGE OF POPULATION, 1880–1920

1880	13.3
1890	14.7
1900	13.6
1910	14.7
1920	13.2

Source: U.S. Census data

In a frontierless democracy, some kind of restriction on immigration was probably not only inevitable but desirable. More and more the question became not *whether* but *how* immigration should be reduced. Most frequently the calls for restriction were accompanied by a denigration of the immigrants themselves. The reformer Robert Hunter, for example, in his important study *Poverty* (1912), wrote that what he called the "evils" of immigration were permanent, not temporary.

> The direct descendants of the people who fought for and defended the Republic and who gave us a rich heritage of democratic institutions, are being replaced by the Slavic, Balkan, and Mediterranean peoples.... In the United States the peasantry from other countries, degraded by foreign oppression, are supplanting the descendants of the original stock of this country. This is race suicide.

Despite increased concern, no major immigration legislation was passed in the years before World War I, though an executive agreement between the United States and Japan did

apply special regulations to the immigration of Japanese. The
most important immigration legislation, passed in 1903 in the
wake of the assassination of President McKinley by Leon
Czolgosz, an American-born anarchist with a foreign name,
prohibited the entry of "anarchists, or persons who believe in
or advocate the overthrow by force and violence of the Government of the United States . . . or the assassination of public
officials." Thus for the first but not the last time, the U.S. government began to inquire into the political beliefs of prospective Americans. Before, when American law barred persons
convicted of certain crimes, it had always stipulated that being
convicted of a political offense in a foreign country not be held
against any prospective immigrant. To be sure, relatively few
persons were kept out of the United States for political reasons
in the early twentieth century, but in the post–World War I
era many immigrants, some of them longtime residents, were
deported for their beliefs.

More significant than legislation were the growth of the immigration service and a massive congressional investigation of
immigration. The immigration bureaucracy grew enor-
mously. In 1891, when an immigration service was first established, the superintendent of immigration had twenty-seven
subordinates. By the end of fiscal 1906 a commissioner general
of immigration supervised more than twelve hundred employees, many of them charged with the operation of the immigration station on Ellis Island, which opened in 1892.
   Partly to remove the immigration question from the 1908
election and partly because it was a typically progressive way
of handling matters, Roosevelt suggested that Congress create
a commission to investigate immigration. In 1907 Congress
created the United States Immigration Commission, whose
massive report published in 1911, in forty-one fact-packed

volumes, remains the largest study of American immigration ever conducted. The commission's conclusions, however, did not always rest upon the facts that its experts—most of whom were middle-class reformers—presented.

Among other things, the commission popularized, if it did not invent, the categories of "old" and "new" immigrants, categories that are still enshrined in almost every American history textbook. Here is an all-too-typical description of the differences between "old" and "new" immigrants taken from a contemporary history text:

> Until the 1880s, most immigrants had come from the British Isles and western Europe, chiefly Germany and Scandinavia. They were usually Protestant, except for the Catholic Irish and some Catholic Germans, and boasted a comparatively high rate of literacy. They fit relatively easily into American society.
>
> But in the 1880s the character of the immigrant stream changed drastically. The so-called New Immigrants—Italians, Croats, Slovaks, Greeks, Poles—came from southern and eastern Europe. Many of them worshiped in Orthodox churches and synagogues. Heavily illiterate and impoverished, they lived together in the "Little Italys" and "Little Polands" of the jam-packed cities.

The commission also claimed that these immigrants were, in a sense, exploiting America without becoming a part of it.

> The old immigration movement was essentially one of permanence. The new immigration is very largely one of individuals, a considerable proportion of whom apparently have no intention of permanently changing their residence, their only purpose in coming to America being to temporarily take advantage of the greater wages paid for industrial labor in this country.

This view reflected the commission's major assumptions: (1) that too many immigrants were coming to America, and (2) that most of those arriving in the late nineteenth and early twentieth centuries were both different from and inferior to those who had predominated before the 1880s.

The sources of immigration had indeed changed, as the following table demonstrates, but the commission's assumption that there were polar differences between immigrant groups is misleading. Certainly there are differences, over time, both between and within immigrant groups; but changing conditions within the United States have been most responsible for shaping immigrant flows. The vast majority of immigrants have come and continue to come to the United States because of economic opportunity; the nature of that opportunity has changed markedly over time. Before and just after the Civil War, an agricultural America attracted large numbers of farmers and would-be farmers, and existing transportation networks reached only to western Europe. By the 1880s the growing American manufacturing sector drew large numbers of persons willing to work in the often brutalizing mines, mills, and factories, and expanding transportation networks facilitated departures from almost every part of Europe. The major legal inhibitions to immigration before 1921 came not from American immigration law but from restrictions other nations placed on their citizens and subjects who wished to depart. The most important of these, in an increasingly militarized Europe, were laws requiring that young men complete their compulsory military service before emigrating. These laws were often evaded, and large numbers of immigrants to America were what would later be called "draft dodgers." (Ironically, half a century later many Americans would emigrate to avoid U.S. military service during the war in Vietnam.)

IMMIGRANTS BY REGION OF LAST RESIDENCE, 1820–1920
(percentages)

Region	1820–1860	1861–1900	1901–1920
Northwestern Europe	95	68	41
Southeastern Europe	-	22	44
North America	3	7	6
Asia	-	2	4
Latin America	-	-	4
Other	2	1	1

Source: Author's computation from INS data

A survey of the status of four large immigrant and ethnic groups is perhaps the best way to illustrate the similarities and differences between them and within them. Two of the groups, Germans and Irish, were well established by the mid-nineteenth century, while the other two, Italians and Jews from eastern Europe, mostly came after 1880. If we disregard immigrants from England and their descendants, who attracted so little notice that the leading scholar of English immigration, Charlotte Erickson, has called them "invisible immigrants," Germans were the largest identifiable group. During the "century of immigration," 1820–1924, nearly six million Germans were recorded as entering the United States, and the 1910 census listed nearly eleven million persons, almost 12 percent of the population, as either foreign-born persons whose mother tongue was German or the children of such persons. (The numbers would be still larger, but the census did not count in either of these categories a person with one parent a foreign-born German speaker and the other a native-born person, even if the latter was of German descent.) While the vast majority of persons who were recorded as being of German mother tongue came from Germany, more than 300,000 German speakers came from Austria and Russia and nearly 200,000 from Hungary.*

Germans had been coming to America since the colonial period, in which large numbers of them, almost all Protestants, settled in Pennsylvania. Nineteenth-century German immigrants were of three confessions: most were Protestants, but a large minority were Catholic and a much smaller minority Jewish. These Germans settled chiefly in Northeastern cities south of New England and in Midwestern cities and countryside, particularly but not exclusively in the region called the "German triangle," an area created by drawing lines on a map to connect the cities of Cincinnati, St. Louis, and Milwaukee, each of which became a center of German immigration. Most Germans, whether urban or rural, were seen as having achieved significant economic and social success, though there was a vast gulf between the German-American intellectuals and professionals of, say, New York City and Chicago and the rural residents of German ethnic enclaves such as Stearns County, Minnesota, or New Braunfels, Texas.

German Americans created and maintained the largest cultural apparatus of any American immigrant group. In the 1880s there were, for example, about eight hundred German-language newspapers, some seventy of them dailies. Perhaps even more important for the maintenance of German-American culture was the degree to which teaching in the German language was carried on in both public and parochial

---

*Included in the latter figures were my grandmother and mother; and though they were Jewish, neither would have been so reported in the census which took account of Yiddish and Hebrew languages but did not tally religions. The census began specific enumeration of second-generation immigrants only in 1880, and in the period we are dealing with made no attempt to enumerate the ethnicity of third and later generations.

schools. In many states with large German populations, laws were passed as early as 1839 enabling or requiring instruction in German in public schools whenever a certain percentage of parents asked for it. Parts of some states, notably Ohio, in effect ran two public school systems, one offering instruction in English, the other in German. Not surprisingly, non-German speakers complained. Beginning with laws passed in Illinois and Wisconsin in 1889 and 1890, several states insisted on instruction in English. The Illinois law required that English be taught in all public schools for at least sixteen weeks a year, while the more aggressive Bennett Law in Wisconsin provided that schools not teaching reading, writing, arithmetic, and American history in the English language were not to be recognized as schools. The Wisconsin law was an attack on both Lutheran and Catholic parochial schools, many of which taught entirely in German, as it meant that attending such schools did not satisfy the state's compulsory attendance law.

The other issue that most divided German Americans from many of their neighbors was Prohibition. Most German Americans, regardless of confession, opposed Prohibition and were advocates of the "continental" as opposed to the "Puritan" Sunday. Although Germans went to the polls relatively united on such issues, the group did not reap as many political plums as its incidence in the population might suggest. Despite local resentment against German "bloc-voting" and other cultural clashes, most nativists on the national scene did not mean Germans when they spoke of undesirable immigrants, and many German Americans participated in the movement to restrict "undesirable" immigration.

The other long-established visible ethnic group was the Catholic Irish, who began coming to the United States in significant numbers in the 1820s and 1830s. Immigration data show more than 5.4 million persons emigrating from Ireland in the century of immigration, about 4.5 million of whom came directly to the United States. Uncounted others crossed the Irish Sea to Britain, so that many of those listed as British in the American immigration data were really second- and third-generation Irish Britons. Unlike Germany, which was uniting politically and growing economically, Ireland was unfree until 1921 and in terrible economic condition. Its population declined by nearly half between 1851 and 1891, from 8.2 million to 4.7 million, so that more people left Ireland in the nineteenth century than remained in it.

The Irish were mainly poor and unskilled; in fact, during the terrible years of famine in the late 1840s the British government "assisted" Irish emigration—one official called the process "shovelling out paupers"—and most Irish emigrants of those years could be considered refugees. Because most Irish immigrants were quite poor and because Irish agricultural conditions were so unlike those in America, few settled in rural areas. Most Irish lived in Eastern cities between Boston and Baltimore, though a sizable minority settled in the same Midwestern cities that attracted Germans.

In the years before the famine, Irish immigration was predominantly male; Irish laborers were crucial in creating the basic infrastructure—canals and railroads—of nineteenth-century America. In the famine years, and for decades afterward, Irish immigration was primarily family migration, and after 1880 more women than men migrated to America from Ireland. Irish women at first worked mainly as domestics, but in the twentieth century more and more became factory and office workers and schoolteachers.

As English-speakers the Irish had no need for the vast formal cultural apparatus constructed by Germans. Their great cultural creation was what some scholars call the Irish Roman Catholic church in America. It became, as Jay P. Dolan has noted, a veritable ethnic fortress for many if not most Irish Catholic Americans, a fortress in which Catholics of other ethnicities could not always find comfortable sanctuary. A relatively high percentage of American Irish chose religious vocations while many others became policemen, so that the Irish-American priest and the Irish-American cop became cultural stereotypes. In fact, Irish Americans filled the ranks of policemen, firemen, horsecar drivers, and other urban occupations. Unlike German artisans or Scandinavian farmers, who did in the New World pretty much what they had done in the Old, the Irish had to adapt, had to fill these economic niches that were developing just as the Irish were settling in American cities.

By the turn of the century Irish-American politicians had achieved great success in many American cities. Most Irish came to America with some understanding of electoral politics; that and the double discrimination from which they suffered as Catholics and as Irish helped to give Irish-American communities strong incentives to gain political power, a power that long remained confined primarily in local politics. No Irish-American politician before Alfred E. Smith, who was first elected governor of New York in 1918, achieved the national prominence of the German-born politicians Carl Schurz, who was secretary of the interior in the Hayes administration, or John P. Altgeld, who was governor of Illinois from 1893 to 1897.

More recent immigrant groups present profiles quite different from those of the Germans, Irish, and other earlier arriving groups. By the twentieth century these latter had second and third generations which outnumbered the first, while among the more recent groups the immigrant generation was still numerically dominant.

Between 1880 and 1920 more than 4 million Italians were

counted entering the United States. No other immigrant group arrived in such numbers in so few years. To be sure, some Italians had come early in American history—one thinks of Lorenzo da Ponte, Mozart's librettist, who taught Italian at Columbia University and tried to establish a permanent opera company in America—but they were relatively few. Before 1870 fewer than 30,000 Italians had come to America; more than 50,000 came in the 1870s, 300,000 in the 1880s, 650,000 in the 1890s, and in the first ten years of the century more than 2 million arrived. Before 1880 most came from northern Italy; afterward immigrants from provinces south of Rome predominated.

Italy, not united politically until 1870, was a land of high population density and very uneven economic development. Its southern provinces were desperately poor, what Italians call *la miseria*. Italy in this era was a classic country of emigration, much of it temporary emigration. One estimate has it that between 1871 and 1971, 26 million Italians emigrated and 13 million of them returned. Unlike the other three groups discussed here, the bulk of whose emigrants came to the United States, Italians also migrated heavily within Europe and to North Africa and South America.

Italian immigration to the United States was highly male, about 75 percent, and was marked by a high remigration rate, perhaps 45 percent. Relatively large numbers came more than once: one survey at Ellis Island showed that some 10 percent of incoming Italians said they had been in the United States before. Of those who stayed in America, perhaps 70 percent settled in the cities of the Northeast, though there was a sizable community in California, mostly of northern Italians, who were important in the development of the fishing industry as well as viniculture and other agricultural enterprises. The majority in the eastern United States, like the Irish before them, did much of the pick-and-shovel work creating new infrastructure: paving urban streets, building elevated lines and bridges, and digging tunnels for subways, trains, and automobile traffic. Although married Italian-American women of the first and second generation rarely worked outside the household, their unmarried daughters did so to a very high degree. One study reported that in New York City just before World War I, 91 percent of unmarried Italian-American women over fourteen years of age were employed. Large numbers of these were in the garment industry, where they supplied perhaps a third of the female labor force in what was otherwise a Jewish industry.

Although overwhelmingly Catholic, Italian Americans had a very different relationship to the Roman Catholic church than did the Irish. The reasons for this lay partly in Italy, partly in America. Whereas in Ireland the church functioned as a protector of Irish against British oppression, in much of pre-1870 Italy the church was the state, and after 1870 the church tended to identify with landlords rather than with the peasantry from which most of the immigrants came. Thus Italians, particularly Italian men, developed an almost reflexive anticlericalism. In America they found an Irish-dominated church which was usually indifferent and sometimes openly hostile to their form of religion. Many fewer Italian-American men than Irish-American men chose the priesthood, and they were much less likely to send their children to parochial schools. A community aphorism, obviously exaggerated, insists that most Italian-American men went to church only three times in their lives: to be hatched, matched, and dispatched, that is, to be baptized, married, and buried.

But as Robert Orsi has described brilliantly in his book *The Madonna of 115th Street*, men participated enthusiastically in the annual festivals held to celebrate the feast day of the particular madonna or patron saint that had been celebrated in that part—often a very tiny part—of Italy from whence they had come. That was possible because the American settlement patterns of many Italians resulted in groupings based on the hometown or village of the migrants. Thus while outsiders looking at the Italian neighborhood of New York saw only a "Little Italy" on the Lower East Side, insiders knew that persons from Palermo tended to live in one area, while another, perhaps just down the block or around the corner, was home to Neapolitans. This was not true only for large cities. One scholar, studying upstate New York, has traced the migration of many families from one Sicilian small town, Valledolmo, to another small town, Fredonia, in Chautauqua County. In these and other ways Italian Americans reinvented forms of what in Italy is called *campanilismo*, the notion that the only people with whom one has real affinity, outside the family, are persons who live within earshot of the local bell tower, the campanile, which exists in every Italian small town. This was reinforced by the high degree of chain migration practiced by Italian and other immigrants. The Italian immigrant's comment, noted earlier, about a friend in America who had sent for him, describes a process that had been going on since the seventeenth century and continues today.

Italians and others who lived in their own ethnic enclaves often had little contact with non-Italian Americans. One immigrant remembering, years later, his boyhood in Little Italy, told an interviewer: "The household my parents established on Mott Street [on the Lower East Side] was typical of those of little Italy. We spoke only Italian, ate Italian food, celebrated Italian holidays, and on Sundays entertained relatives and friends. We knew nothing of the outside world. . . ."

The history of other ethnic groups arriving in this era rings changes on the themes described above. On the surface there may seem to be few similarities between Italians and the Jews of eastern Europe, but in the United States their histories are in some ways remarkably similar. Jews began migrating to the New World long before the United States existed. The first Jews we can identify north of Mexico were 23 persons who came to New York from Brazil in 1654. In the colonial period, Jews largely of Sephardic—that is Iberian—heritage were numbered only in the hundreds. As noted above, Jewish immigrants of German culture were a significant minor part of nineteenth-century migration to the United States, so that by 1880 there were perhaps 250,000 American Jews, five-sixths of them of German heritage. Most of the other sixth were from eastern Europe. By 1920 there were some 4 million American Jews, five-sixths of them eastern European Jews who were largely recent immigrants and their children from the Russian, German, and Austro-Hungarian empires. (A great number came from Poland, which at the time was partitioned among the three empires.)

Like most other Europeans, the eastern Europeans came in search of economic opportunity, but many were also impelled to leave by vicious anti-Semitism officially inspired by the tsarist Russian government. Between 1880 and 1920 perhaps a third or more of the Jews of eastern Europe migrated, and 90 percent of them came to the United States, primarily in family groups. Females represented more than 40 percent, and some 14 percent were children under fourteen. It is believed that fewer than 5 percent returned to Europe, a lower figure than for any other group. New York City, a magnet for most European ethnic groups, was particularly attractive to Jews regardless of their European origin. By 1920 an estimated 45 percent of American Jews lived there. In 1910 about 1.25 million Jews lived on the Lower East Side alone.

Although the German and eastern European Jews shared a

religion, their cultures were not only different but also often antagonistic. In New York one spoke of "uptown Jews" (Germans) and "downtown Jews" (eastern Europeans). The uptown Jews had come speaking German, and they rather easily acculturated to American or German-American life. Many of them had become adherents of Reform Judaism, and the synagogues of the uptown Jews came more and more to resemble American Protestant churches, with relatively large congregations, and were often located on fashionable streets. The downtown Jews came speaking Yiddish (really a variant of German but usually written in Hebrew characters), which many uptown Jews regarded as a jargon. Most downtown Jews had a difficult time adjusting to the patterns of American life, as the classic immigrant novel Abraham Cahan's *The Rise of David Levinsky* (1917) strikingly illustrates. The synagogues of the downtown Jews tended to be small and shabby and located in immigrant neighborhoods, as the orthodox were not allowed to ride on the Sabbath. The membership of many synagogues was restricted to persons who came from the same small eastern European village, or shtetl.

There was much conflict within the Jewish community, between uptown and downtown Jews, but a good deal of cooperation as well, much of it, to be sure, somewhat condescending on the one side, somewhat resentful on the other. Representatives of both groups served on the elite, oligarchical American Jewish Committee. Founded in 1906, it was the first organization to speak effectively for American Jews on such matters as immigration restriction, and to press the American government to protest the mistreatment of Jews in foreign countries, notably tsarist Russia. By this time the United States contained the second largest Jewish community in the world. Seven years later a Jewish fraternal organization, the International Order of B'nai B'rith, created the Anti-

Defamation League expressly to combat anti-Semitism. Social and economic discrimination against Jews, brought over from Europe, had been present in America since colonial times, but only as the numbers of Jews began to grow in the late nineteenth century did anti-Semitic propaganda and activities become a significant aspect of American nativism. Fear of anti-Semitism helped persuade German-American Jewish leaders to defend their coreligionists from eastern Europe ("riffraff," some leaders called them) and to improve their image and status through Americanization.

Although we can see in retrospect that American nativism was building during the Progressive Era, leaders of Euro-American ethnic groups could congratulate themselves that no general restrictive immigration laws had been enacted in the years before the outbreak of World War I. The only real nativist victory came against Japanese immigrants.

Japanese began immigrating to the American mainland in significant numbers shortly after the 1882 passage of the Chinese Exclusion Act. Many of them came after first working on Hawaiian sugar plantations, whose American owners had begun recruiting them as early as 1868, while others came direct from Japan. By 1900 there were about 25,000 Japanese in the country, and by 1910 almost three times that number. Judged by the scale of contemporary European immigration, this was a very small number indeed, but, like the Chinese before them, the Japanese were concentrated on the West Coast, with more than half of them in California. While initially most Japanese worked at menial and low-paying urban and agricultural occupations, many soon became successful farmers. This produced reactions very similar to those which had been created by Chinese immigration: a demand for exclusion based both on economic competition and racist resentment of

nonwhites. Had Japan been a weak nation, as China was in
the nineteenth and early twentieth centuries, there is little
doubt that some kind of Japanese exclusion legislation would
have passed Congress in the first decade of the twentieth century.

But Japan was not a weak nation. Its emergence as a military power of some substance (it had defeated Russia in the
war of 1904–1905) made responsible leaders in Washington
leery of insulting the sensitive Japanese government. President
Theodore Roosevelt, for example, complained privately about
the "idiots" of the California legislature who had passed anti-
Japanese resolutions. TR publicly claimed, after nonlethal
anti-Japanese rioting in San Francisco, that "the mob of a single city may at any time perform acts of lawless violence
which would plunge us into war." (One searches Roosevelt's
papers and addresses in vain for similar denunciations of
antiblack rioting in such places as Atlanta and Springfield;
those riots had no serious international implications.)

The Japanese government, for its part, was chiefly concerned not with its emigrants but with its international status,
which it felt would be damaged by a Japanese exclusion act.
Japanese officials in the United States sought to improve the
image of Japanese immigrants and to move them to behave
"properly" by Western standards. Diplomatic negotiations in
1907–1908 produced the "Gentleman's Agreement," an executive agreement between the United States and Japan which,
unlike a treaty, did not require approval by the U.S. Senate. In
it the United States agreed not to pass discriminatory legislation against Japanese immigrants and to try to stop individual
states from discriminating; Tokyo agreed to stop issuing passports for Japanese laborers bound for the United States. Both
sides agreed that those Japanese "laborers who have already
been in America and [their] parents, wives and children"

might continue to receive passports, which the United States would honor. This last provision meant that Japanese immigration, which had been very heavily male, soon became essentially female. In the ensuing sixteen years some twenty thousand Japanese women were able to come to America and provide the basis for a growing second generation, which of course further aroused nativists.

The Gentlemen's Agreement neither ended anti-Japanese agitation nor sheltered Japanese immigrants and their children from legal, economic, and social abuse. Under federal naturalization law, Japanese, along with other Asians, were "aliens ineligible to citizenship," so they were permanent aliens and thus unable to vote, serve on juries, become lawyers, and so forth. Their native-born children, of course, were protected by the Fourteenth Amendment—"all persons born ... in the United States ... are citizens"—but they too suffered the social and economic restrictions that law and custom inflicted on Asian Americans on the West Coast. They could not, for example, swim in most municipal swimming pools and had to sit in segregated sections of theaters. Beginning in 1913, Western legislators used the "aliens ineligible to citizenship" statutes to frame laws designed to prevent Japanese and other Asians from owning land. And, as one would expect, few non-Japanese employers would hire Japanese of either generation for anything but menial work.

The anti-Japanese agitation surely added strength to the growing consensus that something must be done about immigration. In the midst of a minor frenzy over the passage of an anti-Japanese alien land act by the California legislature and Tokyo's protests about it, Congress again passed the immigrant literacy test in 1913 after a sixteen-year hiatus. President Taft's veto, stressing the country's need for immigrant labor, was sustained, and the movement for general immigration restriction was again stymied. But some kind of broad immigration restriction would likely have been passed in the first quarter of the twentieth century even without World War I. As it was, the war affected almost every aspect of American society, immigration included.

3

World War I and the Ambiguities of Nationalism

WHEN WHAT BECAME World War I began in the summer of 1914 few persons in the United States understood, as Sir Edward Grey, the British foreign minister, put it, that "the lights [were] going out all over Europe." Most American English-language newspapers carried little foreign news, and the assassination of the Austrian Archduke Franz Ferdinand and his wife in Sarajevo by a Serbian "patriot," and subsequent events, were little noted in them. But what had seemed to be just another Balkan skirmish evolved into the first general European war in a century, with the Allies—Britain, France, Russia, and later Italy—on one side and the Central Powers—Germany, Austria-Hungary, and Turkey—on the other. Soon President Woodrow Wilson, in a message to the American people, urged them to "be neutral in thought as well as in deed." This, of course, was impossible. From the very first many old-stock Americans rooted for one side or the other, and many immigrants and their children had deep loyalties to their land of origin. Although direct American involvement seemed out of the question, many Americans sought to profit from the war by selling food, raw materials, and even armaments to the belligerents.

The adherence of the U.S. government to its traditional "freedom of the seas" policy, which held that neutral American ships had the right to move anywhere in international waters, led to conflict with both sets of warring powers. Slowly but surely the United States and Germany, which had never had a serious dispute, edged toward war. The United States declared it in April 1917, nearly three years after the European conflict had begun. It is clear that astute and well-managed British propaganda about the war, including deliberately fabricated atrocity stories, such as one that described how Germans crucified a Canadian soldier or soldiers, had a significant if not precisely definable effect on American opinion. This particular canard chose a Canadian, rather than a British or French soldier, assuming that Americans would have more sympathy for a fellow North American. Note that the story had the Germans performing the classic anti-Christian ritual to emphasize their "otherness" in relation to Western civilization, and the phrase "crucified Canadian" was alliterative and easy to remember. (Some scholars believe that the ready acceptance of these atrocity stories, later proved false, was a factor in the unwillingness of many in the early 1940s to believe the real atrocities of the Holocaust until the end-of-war liberation of Nazi concentration camps provided unmistakable evidence of the horrors committed by the Nazi regime.)

While these World War I horror stories which depicted the Germans as bestial and subhuman played a part in swinging American public opinion to support American intervention, other factors, including economic advantage, submarine warfare, and German diplomatic stupidity, had greater effect. But the steady diet of anti-German propaganda in the years before the United States entered the war surely paved the way for the nativism directed at Germans and German Americans that flourished in the years after 1917.

American participation in World War I and in the preparedness drive that preceded it heightened both American nationalism and nativism. It not only increased existing tensions between some ethnic and racial groups and the larger society but provided opportunities for members of most groups to improve their condition, as such crises usually do. The British historian Arthur Marwick has analyzed what he calls the "participation dimension" of modern wars, which "more and more involve the participation of hitherto underprivileged groups in the community [who] tend to benefit from such participation." This was certainly true to a degree in American society, but in World War I America, as opposed to World War II America, the negative effects were, in the final analysis, more pervasive than the positive.

The first noticeable effects of the war in the United States after August 1914 were a decline in economic activity, a sharp drop-off in immigration, and a shifting of its sources. Not only was it increasingly difficult for Europeans to emigrate, but many recent young male immigrants to the United States were infused with sufficient patriotism to return to their native lands to fight. This slackening of immigration meant that, in 1915 and after, when the war orders first of the Allied powers and then of the American preparedness and war programs created an economic boom, manufacturers and other businesses had to recruit new workers from the ranks of African Americans, Mexican immigrants, and, to a lesser degree, women.

One might imagine that, given the drop in immigration, pressures for immigration restriction would also have declined, but such was not the case. In the last prewar year—

July 1, 1913, to June 30, 1914—immigration totaled some 1.2 million persons, nearly 90 percent of it from Europe. Two years later the total had fallen to 300,000, with fewer than half from Europe. In addition, more than 125,000 persons left the country, so net immigration for the year 1915–1916 was just over 150,000.

In spite of this reduced immigration, Congress passed the immigrant literacy test again in both 1915 and 1917. Wilson vetoed it both times, stressing, as he was wont to do, moral issues. He noted that immigrants came seeking opportunity and that the bill would reject them "unless they already had one of the chief of the opportunities they seek, the opportunity of education." The president's 1915 veto was sustained by just four votes in the House. Two years later it was a different story. At a time of rising nationalism and rapidly deteriorating relations with Germany, Congress overwhelmingly overrode the president's veto, 287 to 106 in the House and 62 to 19 in the Senate. That a popular president with majorities in both houses could be so little regarded by Congress just three months after his reelection is testimony to the strength of anti-immigrant feeling. And, it must be noted, Wilson himself had contributed to that feeling in his writings as a popular historian and by his attacks on "hyphenated Americans" during his preparedness campaign.

Although the law enacted in 1917 was the first significant general restriction of immigration ever passed, it might be well to recapitulate the restrictive acts passed once the Chinese exclusion legislation had established a precedent. The first but ineffective piece of restrictive legislation had actually preceded the 1882 exclusion act: an 1875 statute had barred the entry of "women for the purpose of prostitution" and criminals "whose sentence [had] been remitted on condition of emigration." In 1885 and 1887 laws forbidding the entry of contract laborers were enacted. In 1891 new categories of excluded persons were created: "all idiots, insane persons, paupers or persons likely to become a public charge, persons suffering from a loathsome or dangerous contagious disease, persons who have been convicted of a felony or other infamous crime or misdemeanor involving moral turpitude, [and] polygamists." (The last category was directed against Mormons, not Muslims.) In 1903, in the wake of McKinley's assassination, Congress added to the categories of persons barred "anarchists, or persons who believe in or advocate the overthrow by force and violence of the Government of the United States . . . or the assassination of public officials."

The 1917 law required that all future adult immigrants would have to be literate, though in the case of family immigration, if the husband were literate the wife need not be. The American test, unlike its two British Commonwealth predecessors, was a fair one. As opposed to the Natal Act (1897), which required literacy in English, and the "White Australia Act" (1901), which required literacy in any language chosen by the examiner, the 1917 law defined literacy as being able to read any recognized language, including Hebrew and Yiddish. Extreme nativists wanted an "English only" law, but that never received serious congressional consideration. Another provision of the 1917 act created a "barred zone," described in degrees of longitude and latitude, barring immigrants from all of Asia except China, Japan, and the Philippines. For practical purposes this chiefly affected immigrants from India, of whom there were perhaps ten thousand already in the United States. (Most Chinese and Japanese were already effectively barred by other laws and regulations, and the courts ruled that Filipinos, as "United States nationals," could not be kept out, but neither could they become naturalized citizens.) Other provisions, by adding criteria, expanded the kinds of mental, physical, and moral "defects" that were grounds for exclusion, and made the existing antiradical provisions, first adopted in 1903, more severe.

Despite all the struggle it occasioned, the literacy test, when finally enacted, had little effect. During the last year of which it was the major statutory bar to immigration (July 1920–June 1921), more than 800,000 immigrants entered the country and 250,000 returned home. About 1.5 percent of all entrants, nearly 14,000 persons, were excluded or deported on one ground or another. Only a tenth of these, a mere 1,450 persons, were kept out by the literacy test. Rising standards of education in Europe had pulled most of the teeth from the law; had it been enacted when first proposed in the 1880s, it would have been more effective. Despite its eventual uselessness as a deterrent, the passage of the literacy test was an important nodal point for the movement to restrict immigration. It showed the restrictionists that they could command majority support, and the law's obvious failure to restrict was used as an added argument that something more needed to be done.

In addition to strengthening the antiradical provisions of immigration law, the 1917 act for the first time made the espousal of certain kinds of radicalism or immoral or criminal behavior by immigrants within five years *after* they came to America, grounds for deportation, and extended the time limit for retroactive deportation under the "LPC clause" from one to five years. The numbers of persons deported was never a significant percentage of immigrants—only in 1926 were as many as ten thousand persons deported in one year, and not until 1948 were as many as twenty thousand so deported—but the desire of congressional majorities to expel persons thought undesirable was symptomatic of the whole nativist complex.

With the passage of the 1917 act, U.S. immigration policy

had been restricted in eight distinct ways in the thirty-five years since the first Chinese Exclusion Act. The excluded categories included contract laborers; Asians (except for certain Chinese and Japanese, and all Filipinos); certain criminals; persons who failed to meet certain moral standards, primarily concerned with prostitution; persons with certain diseases; paupers; some radicals; and illiterates.

Administrative manipulation of the law by immigration officials and their superiors is crucial to an understanding of how the laws have actually affected the ebb and flow of immigrants. Within weeks of the passage of the 1917 law, growers in the American Southwest began to urge the government to exempt Mexicans from the law's provisions because they feared a farm labor shortage. Mexican laborers were particularly prized by Western growers because they were close at hand, cheap, and would return home after the growing season. Many growers, such as C. C. Teague, president of the California Fruit Growers Exchange, believed that Mexicans were "naturally adapted to agricultural work, particularly in the handling of fruits and vegetables ... loyal and faithful, good-natured and happy." Secretary of Labor William B. Wilson, mindful of the wartime need for food production— "Food Can Win the War" was a popular slogan—soon issued orders that Mexican agricultural laborers be exempted from literacy tests, head taxes, and other restrictions of the new immigration laws.

For American Indians the impact of the war was probably more positive than negative, though contemporaries and some scholars have often overstated the benefits. Wilson's commissioner of Indian affairs, Cato Sells, in a 1918 article fantasized that the war would be "the beginning of the end of the Indian problem" and that Indians would fight "side by side with the white man, not as Indians but as Americans. ... gaining by

contact an education that will lead them away from the tribal
relations, and give them a definite comprehension of the genius of American institutions."

Many Indians were able to benefit from expanded wartime
opportunities and left their reservations for urban areas, pre-
figuring a much larger migration during World War II. Even
more important was the military service of perhaps as many as
ten thousand Indians. Although all Indian males between
twenty-one and thirty-one years of age had to register for the
draft, only citizen Indians could be drafted. Before the passage
of the Dawes Act in 1887, Indians were not citizens. That act
conferred citizenship only on those Indians who had been
granted lands in severalty. This meant that anywhere from
one-half to two-thirds of all registered Indians, as noncitizens,
were not draft eligible. Approximately 75 percent of those
who served enlisted rather than being drafted. Perhaps four
thousand Indians in the military were from the Five Civilized
Tribes of Oklahoma. After the war Congress conferred citizenship on all honorably discharged Indian veterans if they
formally requested it, and in 1924 all Indians born in the
United States were declared citizens. Throughout the period
covered by this book, Indians, although citizens, were almost
universally denied the right to vote by those Western states in
which most of them lived.

Despite the continuing stereotype of all Indians as traditional warriors—"natural-born scouts," as one enthusiast put
it—there were great differences in the responses of various
tribes. A high percentage of Cheyenne and Arapaho young
men enlisted or were drafted, but probably not more than a
dozen of the numerous Navajos did. On a few reservations the
draft registration sparked unrest, immediately attributed by
some whites to "German agents," who were nonexistent on
the desolate reservations.

On the other hand the wartime fervor of Americanism seemed to heighten the drive of Bureau of Indian Affairs officials to force assimilation on Indians, so much so that Donald Parman has styled World War I as "the war to assimilate all Indians." The BIA accelerated the process by which Indians could gain control of individual plots of land, and, as often had been the case in the past, the overwhelming majority of those who got land soon lost it. Some Indians who had received "fee patented" land while in military service returned home after the war to find that their land had been sold for nonpayment of taxes.

For African Americans the war seemed to open great opportunities, economic and social. The absence of immigrants created jobs and encouraged what has been called the "great migration" of many blacks from the South to the North. While some of that migration was spurred by labor recruiters employed by Northern employers, much, perhaps most of it, was the result of the same kind of "chain migration" of relatives and friends that had drawn Italians and other Europeans across the Atlantic. Some African-American newspapers that circulated in the South, such as the *Chicago Defender*, also urged blacks to abandon the region.

It has been estimated that some 750,000 blacks left the South for the North during and just after World War I, which greatly increased the African-American population of the Middle Atlantic and Midwestern states. Perhaps most dramatic was the influx to Chicago. The census of 1920 reported more than 100,000 blacks in the city, an almost 150 percent increase in its resident black population since 1910. New York City's larger population grew more slowly but nonetheless increased by more than two-thirds to just over 150,000. Dozens of other Northern cities saw African-American population growth rates of more than 50 percent. Although this migra-

tion was an important development, and one that would continue unevenly for most of the twentieth century, concentration on it too often obscures the fact that the overwhelming
majority of America's more than 10 million African Americans, some 85 percent, continued to live in the South. The
state of Georgia alone had more blacks—1.2 million—than
did all the Middle Atlantic and East North Central states
combined.

While many employers were recruiting African Americans
for industrial jobs, white workers and their unions in the
North were almost uniformly hostile to their coming. This
hostility sometimes erupted into brutal violence. The worst
such outbreak occurred in East St. Louis, Illinois, during the
first three days of July 1916. Employers of East St. Louis had
recruited blacks not only to fill vacant jobs but also to serve as
strikebreakers in labor disputes. Egged on by some union
leaders and newspapers—a headline in one local paper read
"Make East St. Louis a Lily White Town"—the hostility
boiled over into mob violence as whites used a Sunday to drive
through the black part of town, firing into residences. Armed
African Americans defended themselves, and before the car-
nage ended at least forty-eight persons had been killed, forty
of them black. By some estimates at least $400,000 worth of
property was destroyed, most of it owned by African Americans. Perhaps even more shocking than the riot itself was the
response of many whites to it. Samuel Gompers, for example,
president of the American Federation of Labor, defended the
white rioters as protectors of their jobs and families. A special
congressional committee appointed to investigate the East St.
Louis riots, although critical of the rioters and the local administration of justice, nevertheless began its report by speaking of the "natural racial aversion" between whites and blacks.

Later that month, in one of the first large peaceful demonstrations by blacks—what we would call today a civil rights demonstration—between ten and fifteen thousand African Americans marched silently along Fifth Avenue in New York City to protest the East St. Louis and other race riots and

> because we are thoroughly opposed to Jim Crow cars, segregation, discrimination, disfranchisement, lynching, and the host of evils that are forced upon us. It is time that the spirit of Christ should be manifested in the making and execution of laws.
>
> We march because we want our children to live in a better land and enjoy fairer conditions than have fallen to our lot.

About 400,000 African-American men served in the U.S. army during World War I, perhaps half of them in France and some 42,000 as combat troops. While most were led by white officers, more than a thousand black men became commissioned officers (less than 1 percent of all officers), most of them trained at the all-black officers' training school at Fort Des Moines, Iowa. (Until the Korean War in the 1950s, the army adhered to a policy of strict racial segregation, and most black soldiers were utilized as stevedores, cooks, and laborers.) Many of those who fought as infantry in World War I were assigned to fight with French divisions, and many all-black units, such as the 369th Infantry, served with distinction. Henry Johnson and Needham Roberts, the first Americans to be awarded the Croix de Guerre, France's highest military decoration for bravery, were African-American enlisted men.

Despite this and other patriotic service, black soldiers were routinely abused and sometimes murdered in the United States. Before the war there had been a long history of such abuse in Southern states, particularly Texas. For example, the Brownsville, Texas, riot of 1906 occurred when, responding to

the abuse of some of their comrades by police, black soldiers illegally seized their weapons and headed to town, killing a bar-
tender and seriously wounding a Mexican-American
lieutenant of police in the resulting melee. Although only
some of the soldiers stationed there had been involved, President Theodore Roosevelt ordered the dishonorable discharge
of an entire battalion of black troops because none would
identify those who had participated. After a Senate investigation, all qualified soldiers were allowed to reenlist, though
their dishonorable discharges remained on their records. Similar tensions existed between black soldiers and white police
and other civilians throughout the South.

Wartime, supposedly a time of unity and shared sacrifice,
did not ease these tensions. The most serious racial distur-
bance of the war years occurred in Houston, Texas, on August
23, 1917. Following a long series of incidents between white
Houston police officers and black soldiers, what should have
been a minor affair—the arrest and physical abuse of two
black soldiers who tried to intervene in the arrest of a black
woman—became a tragedy. At Camp Logan on the outskirts
of the city, where the troops were stationed, soldiers came to
believe that a black soldier had been murdered by the police.
That evening a number of soldiers armed themselves—some
reports say more than a hundred of the several hundred
black soldiers stationed at Logan—and went into Houston
vowing revenge on the police. One newspaper later reported
the soldiers' rallying cry as "To hell with going to France,
let's clean up this dirty town." During a night of violence thirteen persons were killed. Only one of them was an African-
American—a highly unusual statistic in American race riots.
At least nineteen persons were seriously wounded, five of
whom were black soldiers. Just 110 days later, on December
11, 1917, thirteen of the soldiers involved were hanged. By

that time forty-one other soldiers had been sentenced to life imprisonment, four others to shorter terms, and five had been acquitted.

East St. Louis and Houston were merely the flash points along the color line, places where, for a variety of reasons, the heightened racial antagonisms of the war years, clearly worsened by whites seeing blacks doing what were regarded as "white" jobs or wearing the national uniform, burst into fatal violence. In the years after the war, particularly during what African Americans learned to call the "red summer" of 1919, these tensions grew even worse.

The war years also strengthened the attack on immigrant cultures, usually disguised under the rubric of "Americanization." The same cultural forces that had produced the upsurge of nativism, created the Dillingham commission, and led to increasing congressional regulation of immigration were also important in the creation of the Americanization movement, one of the less studied aspects of progressivism. The Dillingham commission had noted that in 1909 more than half—57.8 percent—of the children in the nation's thirty-seven largest cities were either immigrants or, more often, the children of immigrants. In some cities—New York, for example—the figure was closer to three-quarters. During much of the nineteenth century the public schools had performed many Americanizing functions, mostly by teaching immigrant children the English language and by the bits of American history and civics that were part of the curriculum; but immigrant children were not a major concern of most American educators in that era.

Between 1914 and 1921 what some scholars have called the "Americanization Movement" flourished. It was an organized campaign to insure political loyalty and cultural conformity and enjoyed the support of most state governments and three federal agencies: the Bureau of Education, the Bureau of Naturalization, and, after its establishment in 1917, the Committee on Public Information. Americanization programs ordinarily involved a complex process of socialization which went far beyond instruction in English and civics to include training in personal cleanliness, middle-class values, and discipline more appropriate to the factory than to the classroom. In many if not most cases, disdain for the immigrant heritage was deliberately instilled in the children of the foreign-born by the organized programs of the war years and after.

Some of those involved in the Americanization movement were genuinely interested in helping immigrants and especially their children adjust to American life, but even they almost always did so in a paternalistic manner. Like their contemporaries, many were genuinely alarmed about the immigrant majority in so many big-city public schools, where large numbers of pupils began their education without even a rudimentary knowledge of English. In Chicago this was more than two-thirds of the pupils, and in New York City the figure was more than seven of ten. Frances Kellor, founder of a Committee for Immigrants in America, and Julia Richman are good examples of that kind of progressive reformer. Richman, a German Jewish American who became district superintendent of New York's Lower East Side schools during the first decade of the twentieth century, used methods that seem harsh today. She laid down rules that forbade students from using Yiddish and other foreign languages in school, even during recess or in the toilets, and encouraged her teachers to punish offending students by washing their mouths out with soap.

Other Americanizers, perhaps more numerous, were openly hostile to immigrants. Most adhered to the "melting pot approach," which saw immigrant culture as something to be boiled away, as impurities are boiled away in making steel. To be sure, the coiner of the "melting pot" metaphor, the European playwright Israel Zangwill, had insisted that "the process of American amalgamation is not assimilation or simple surrender to the dominant type, as is popularly supposed, but an all-round give-and-take by which the final type may be enriched or impoverished," and had his protagonist proclaim, "God is making the American. . . . The real American has not yet arrived." But most of those who borrowed the phrase assumed just the kind of "simple surrender" that Zangwill rejected and believed that immigrant culture had nothing to contribute to American society.

Professor Ellwood P. Cubberley, a progressive reformer and one of the most important spokespersons for professional educators, argued that it was the duty of the schools to "assimilate and amalgamate these people [i.e., immigrants] as a part of our American race, and to implant in their children, so far as can be done, the Anglo-Saxon conception of righteousness, law and order, and popular government." Similarly, two leading social work reformers, Sophonsiba Breckinridge and Edith Abbott, honestly feared that if "children of illiterate immigrant parents cannot be placed in schools soon after their arrival in this country the way to delinquency through dependency is sure to be open to them."

Many social workers and schoolteachers consciously turned children against their immigrant parents. Years later Mario Cuomo wrote of his own experience:

I can cry now when I think about the time when I was fourteen years old and embarrassed to bring my father to St. John's Preparatory School to meet the teachers and other parents because he didn't speak English well. Looking back now, and feeling the anguish of that recollection, teaches me all I need to know about the ethnic self-hate and the melting pot myth and what it means to deny a heritage.

At the other extreme were "scientific racists" such as Professor Edward A. Ross, a leading sociologist who believed, as did many social and physical scientists of the era, that behavioral patterns were hereditary:

> That the Mediterranean peoples are morally below the races of northern Europe is as certain as any social fact. Even when they were dirty, ferocious barbarians, these blonds were truth-tellers. Be it pride or awkwardness or lack of imagination or fair-play sense, something has held them back from the nimble lying of the southern races.

A few advanced thinkers, such as John Dewey, Horace M. Kallen, and Randolph Bourne, wrote of the need to redefine Americanism to mean not a simple exchange of the old immigrant identity for the new American one, but rather the creation of a new identity which partook of some elements of each. Bourne, the most radical and least influential of the three, wrote a brilliant essay in 1916 entitled "Transnational America," in which he scathingly attacked the simplistic melting-pot definition of Americanism and the whole Americanization movement. He called instead for a more cosmopolitan definition which would preserve and nurture immigrant traditions. Some less celebrated writers, such as the immigrant Constantine Panunzio, insisted that "One of the forces which make for Americanization and one which is seldom recognized is found in the very idea of America which the newcomer brings with him. To the average immigrant America is the acme of all dreams."

But these were voices crying in the wilderness. The overwhelming majority of Americans, including more than a few immigrants and their children, believed that assimilation, the abandonment of what some called "Old World traits," was the only way for immigrants to become Americans. Most probably would have approved the pageant staged by the industrialist Henry Ford for his workers. At center stage was a giant cauldron. From one side came immigrant men and women, in varied European peasant costumes, many of the men bearded and many of the women wearing scarves over their heads. To the accompaniment of patriotic music they approached the giant cauldron, climbed stairs on one side of it, and disappeared into it, only to emerge a few minutes later on the other side, now clothed in simple American attire and without beards or headcoverings. The immigrants were now Americans, baptized, so to speak, in the omnipotent melting pot.

It is difficult to make sensible generalizations about the war's effects on immigrant groups because the situations and experiences of the various ethnic groups were so different. Since most immigrants were working people, the increased level of economic activity, especially after mid-1915, was surely a benefit to most. But as American neutrality changed to partisanship and then to intervention, many of those ethnic groups and individuals with close ties to one or the other of the warring powers were caught up in the maelstrom of passions that the war evoked. In addition, many immigrants who had come to America at least in part to avoid the militarism of Europe were puzzled and disturbed when the martial spirit came to prevail in their new home as well.

While more members of immigrant/ethnic groups came to support the Allies rather then the Central Powers, three very large groups—German Americans, Irish Americans, and American Jews—tended to support Germany and its partners in the period before the United States went to war. In exploring these ethnic group loyalties, three points must be kept in

mind. First, to favor one side or the other did not entail disloyalty to the United States before it entered the war in April
1917; second, after that entry all but a very few persons, immigrant or native-born, behaved as patriotic Americans; and
third, the vast majority of persons in the ethnic groups, like
most other Americans, devoted most of their time and energy
to making a living and to living their own lives.

The reasons for support of the Central Powers were quite
different. For German Americans, support of Germany
seemed natural: most continued to have relatively close con-
nections to German culture and were proud of Germany's
achievements since its 1870 unification. Irish Americans had
no particular attachment to Germany, but they opposed England, which they saw as Ireland's oppressive colonial over-
lord, and thus supported England's enemy. The brutal
suppression of the Easter Rebellion of 1916 in Dublin and
elsewhere in Ireland only increased that long-standing antag-
onism. A few Irish Americans, some of them prominent in
Irish-American organizations such as the Ancient Order of
Hibernians, collaborated with agents of the German government in the United States in both legal anti-British propaganda and in activities forbidden by American neutrality law,
such as trying to send weapons to India to foment a rebellion
there against Britain. Much more common was ongoing support of the several varieties of Irish nationalism.

Although persons whose historical memory includes only
the Nazi era and the Holocaust find it difficult to believe,
most organized American Jewish opinion at the onset of
World War I was favorable to Germany. The two main
groups of American Jews had different reasons for their attitudes. For the minority of Jews who were of German origin,
the reasons were the same as for other German Americans.
An influential Chicago rabbi, Benjamin Felsenthal, put forth

a creed which, except for its first sentence, applied to most German Americans of any confession:

> I am a Jew for I have been born among the Jewish nation. Politically I am an American, as patriotic, as enthusiastic, as devoted an American citizen as it is possible to be. But spiritually I am a German, for my inner life has been profoundly affected by Schiller, Goethe, Kant, and other intellectual giants of Germany.

The more numerous American Jews of eastern European origin had no such ties, intellectual or otherwise. For them, and for many German-American Jews as well, tsarist Russia was the major source of anti-Semitism, and its frequent anti-Jewish pogroms, often inspired by the Russian government, made support for Russia abhorrent. For these Jews, like so many Irish, it was important that the Allies not win. Jewish attitudes toward Russia changed somewhat in February 1917 when the first Russian Revolution of that year made it seem, for a while at least, as if democracy might prevail there. After the Bolsheviks made a separate peace with Germany in March 1918, some of the large minority of eastern European Jews who were socialists continued to express antiwar sentiments even though the United States had joined the Allied side.

More ethnic groups were rooting for the Allies. The relatively few German-speaking Austrian Americans tended to support the Central Powers, as did the larger number of Hungarian Americans. But most of the several millions who had come to America from the Austro-Hungarian Empire were members of its subject nations: Poles, Czechs, Slovaks, Southern Slavs, and some Italians. The politically aware minority of these groups, attracted by Woodrow Wilson's promise of "self-determination" for the subject peoples of Europe in his Fourteen Points, supported the Allies. So, of course, did most non-Irish Britons, most French, and, after Italy entered the war on the Allied side, many Italians. Also favoring the Allies were most of the relatively few Japanese Americans, as Japan had gone to war with Germany: a small number of Japanese immigrants served voluntarily in the American armed forces even though they were "aliens ineligible to citizenship."

Millions of Americans of all kinds saw little merit in the European struggle and opposed the war altogether, on a number of grounds. Many if not most Scandinavian Americans took this position, as did many nonimmigrant residents of the Midwestern states, where so many Scandinavians and Germans had settled. Americans living on either coast and in the South were less likely to oppose intervention. Again, it must be noted that probably a majority of recent immigrants were apolitical, and many who were not were radicals who opposed a "capitalist war."

America did intervene, however, and with that intervention the old notion of "My country, right or wrong" came to prevail. But it is necessary to remember that just five months before the United States went to war at President Wilson's urging, Wilson had won a narrow election victory in which the slogan "He Kept Us Out of War" was widely used. The overwhelming majority of immigrants of every ethnic group, like the overwhelming majority of Americans, supported the war—with greater or lesser degrees of enthusiasm. They volunteered for military service, submitted to the draft, bought Liberty Bonds, worked longer hours, conserved food, and did all the patriotic things their government urged them to do.

Many Americans, in and out of government, thought it necessary to create enthusiasm for the war and did so by resorting to hate propaganda. The first United States government propaganda agency, the innocuously titled Committee on Public Information, with 150,000 employees, was created to "sell" the war to the American people. Not only did German soldiers become "Huns," bent on raping women and bayoneting babies, but all things German came under attack.

Some of the results of anti-German phobias were merely foolish: sauerkraut, for example, was renamed "liberty cabbage." The names of many streets were changed: in Cincinnati, for example, German Street became English Street, and Berlin Street became Woodrow Street. More seriously, it became difficult if not impossible for symphony orchestras to play the music of long-dead German composers such as Beethoven and Brahms, and many public libraries took German-language books off their shelves and in some cases destroyed them. Laws in a number of states prohibited the teaching of the German language, and in many states without such laws, high schools, colleges, and even some universities, such as the University of Chicago, canceled their classes in German. While the college courses were soon reinstated, the teaching of foreign languages in American high schools suffered a setback from which it has yet to recover.

Some states forbade the speaking of German in a public place, which meant that even church services in German had to be abandoned. As one Nebraska legislator put it, "If these people are Americans, let them speak our language." The Nebraska legislature passed, and the governor signed, a law that prohibited the teaching of any subject in a language other than English. It also prohibited the study of any foreign language—specifically including Latin—before the eighth grade. After the war these laws were either abandoned or declared unconstitutional by the federal courts, but during the war, as has usually been the case in American history, there was little judicial interference with governmental infringements of traditional American liberties. The courts acted as if the Bill of Rights had enlisted for military service and was no longer available for domestic duty. Only after the war ended did the courts begin to curb wartime excesses. The key case invalidating state laws forbidding foreign-language instruction, *Meyer v. Nebraska*, was decided in 1920.

Both federal and state governments encouraged Americans to be anti-German, and they were abetted by most of the press and the infant but influential motion picture industry, which turned out films with such titles as *The Kaiser, the Beast of Berlin*. Thus it is not surprising that mob violence against German Americans erupted. Mobs forced many German Americans to buy government Liberty Bonds, or to kneel and kiss the American flag, or to undergo other presumed tests of "loyalty." A few were tarred and feathered or subjected to other physical abuse, and at least one German American was lynched by a mob, not in the South but in Illinois.

Although not listed on any official casualty list, German-American high culture, the most prolific non-English culture in America, was severely wounded during the war and never recovered. To be sure, even without the government-inspired cultural terrorism of World War I, its demise was in time all but certain because of the highly successful adaptation of most German Americans to the larger culture. Still, nothing better symbolizes what one scholar called "the tragedy of German America" than what happened to the National German-American Alliance, a federation of some ten thousand clubs with as many as two million members and the largest ethnic organization in prewar America. Once the war broke out, the Alliance devoted most of its energies to keeping America neutral. On April 11, 1918, as all things German or German-American were under heavy attack, the Alliance dissolved itself while issuing a defensive statement that "no act of disloyalty has been proved against" it. The $30,000 left in its treasury it donated to the Red Cross. The wartime ordeal brought the final curtain down prematurely on much of German-American culture. If the cultural disappearance of German Americans has been overstated (minor aspects of German-American culture survived the war and exist today), the day of German Americans as an influential American ethnic group was over.

Coupled with the anti-German hysteria was an extreme antiradicalism aimed at both foreign-born and native radicals. Congress passed, and President Wilson approved, both the Espionage Act of 1917 and the Sedition Act of 1918. These heedless legislative measures, now all but universally condemned by scholars, were ostensibly aimed at spies, saboteurs, and German sympathizers, but the nearly two thousand federal prosecutions under these statutes jailed mainly antiwar socialists, such as native-born Eugene V. Debs, who were not at all pro-German, and members of the Industrial Workers of the World, who were militantly anticapitalist. This antiradicalism received an infusion of energy when, in November 1917, Lenin and the Bolsheviks seized power in Russia and soon agreed to a separate peace with Germany. Lenin was widely depicted as a German agent. Nothing illustrates more clearly how nativist targets switched from Germans to radicals than the history of a witch-hunting United States Senate committee which started out investigating the German-American-dominated brewing industry and German propaganda but switched, after the October Revolution, to an investigation of Bolshevik propaganda!

The end of the war in November 1918 and the rapid demobilization of soldiers and civilian war workers did not diminish nativism and hysteria. The obvious failure of stated American war aims and of the peace settlement at Versailles —American intervention did not, as Wilson had prophesied, make the world safe for democracy—probably increased rather than lessened the antiforeign feelings of most Americans. These antiforeign feelings now came to include not only groups such as the Chinese, or categories such as illiterates, but all aliens and a fairly large proportion of American citizens as well. Fears of foreigners combined with fears of radicalism and racial and religious prejudices in the postwar decade to produce what one historian has called the "tribal twenties."

4

Postwar Passions

AFTER THE FIGHTING in Europe ended with an armistice on November 11, 1918, the ensuing years were a time of great confusion and uncertainty in the United States. Most histories concentrate on the diplomacy and politics of the period. It was then that an American president for the first time went abroad to negotiate with leaders of other countries in what we would now call a "summit." Surely Woodrow Wilson's two round-trips across the Atlantic, his triumphal tour of France, England, and Italy, and negotiations at Versailles with Britain's David Lloyd George, France's Georges Clemençeau, and others, as well as his eventual failure to convince the United States to ratify the treaty that he brought back from Europe, are topics of high drama. In the course of a speaking tour to rally the country behind him, Wilson suffered a stroke and physical collapse in Pueblo, Colorado, on September 25, 1919, and for the remaining seventeen months of his presidency was an invalid largely confined to the White House.

Most ordinary Americans, though aware of these epochal events, were chiefly concerned with other matters. Particularly they sought to readjust their lives from the hectic but essentially prosperous war years to a more orderly but economically precarious peacetime. Many if not most of them

ached for what Wilson's successor in the White House, Warren G. Harding, called "normalcy." But the prewar world
would never return.

No substantial planning had been done, by government or
business, for postwar reconstruction. For example, tens of
thousands of temporary government workers in Washington
were simply dismissed within days after the Armistice and
told not to come to work anymore. They did not even receive
their final paycheck which was due at the end of the month.
Bernard M. Baruch, a millionaire speculator who was one of
Wilson's key wartime economic administrators, tells in his
memoirs how he made temporary loans to many of the persons who worked in his office so they could buy their train
tickets to get back home.

Most of the returning American servicemen found that no
serious planning had been done for them either. Those who
were healthy were quickly discharged and given a mustering-
out payment of sixty dollars, which soon came to be called a
"suit of clothes" bonus. Wounded men and those who had
contracted serious disease while in military service found in-
adequate medical facilities waiting for them once they were
discharged. Concern for the more than 4.5 million returning
veterans became a major political issue for half a dozen years
after the war. In addition, almost 117,000 American soldiers
were never coming home, having been killed in battle or by
disease. This was a small "butcher's bill" compared with the
losses of the major European powers whose dead were numbered in millions, but these "minor losses," as some military
writers describe them, left voids in the lives of thousands of
American families. On top of that, just as the war was ending
the United States was smitten by the great "Spanish" in-
fluenza pandemic, which killed perhaps 20 million persons
worldwide in late 1918 and early 1919, more than 500,000 of

whom were Americans—more than were killed in the entire World War.

This change, confusion, and disorder provided the background for the events of 1919–1921. To be sure, there had been similar forces at work in the country during the war years, but in wartime a common goal—winning the war—appeared to provide most Americans with a unified purpose. No such unity marked the postwar years. Instead Americans were seriously divided over economics, politics, and how they wanted to live their lives. The adoption of two constitutional amendments in 1919 and 1920, prohibiting the sale or manufacture of "intoxicating liquors" and mandating the right of women to vote on the same terms as men, seemingly settled issues that had been debated for years—but they too divided Americans. These divisions, along with disputes over race, religion, and radicalism, it can be argued, had been present throughout most of the previous century; but during the war and particularly in the immediate postwar years and beyond, they achieved a new primacy.

For American Indians, the problems of postwar reconversion were similar to in kind but worse in degree than those of other segments of the population. Most demobilized soldiers and unemployed war workers returned to poverty-stricken reservations even more aware of how much worse off, economically and socially, their condition was than that of most other Americans. For the overwhelming majority of Indians, the immediate postwar years brought not change but more of the same. The white assault on Indian property continued, abetted by state and federal governments. Many entrepreneurs saw Indians as obstacles to Western economic development, especially when some of their seemingly useless reservations were found to contain scarce resources, chiefly oil and natural

gas. These increasing violations, especially when coupled with
massive corruption, ultimately created renewed interest in the
rights of Indians among some white reformers, with resonat-
ing responses from some Indians and Indian tribes.

If a kind of stasis existed for most American Indians,
African Americans endured horrifying experiences in the
postwar era, especially during the "Red Summer" of 1919
when racial disturbances, large and small, left scars on at least
twenty-five American cities. Significant but fewer riots occurred in 1920 and 1921. The riots in Chicago and in Tulsa,
Oklahoma, are important in themselves and can stand as examples of what some scholars have classified as "Northern
style" and "Southern style" disturbances, or, as Gunnar
Myrdal put it in his classic 1944 study, riots in which "Negroes
fight as unreservedly as whites" and riots of "one-way terrorization."

The largest and most destructive of these riots, a "Northern
style" riot, occurred in Chicago in July 1919. As noted,
Chicago was one of the cities most affected by the wartime
"great migration" of Southern blacks to Northern cities. Although, like most Northern cities, Chicago had no segregation
ordinances, residential segregation prevailed, maintained in
part by "restrictive covenants," clauses placed into real estate
titles which limited the sale or transfer of that particular piece
of property to members of certain groups, usually "Cau-
casians," but often "Christians" or "gentiles" or even simply
"Protestants." In western New York some covenants barred
sales to "any Italian." In 1917, in a decision that was not reversed until 1948, the U.S. Supreme Court upheld the en-
forceability of such covenants in state courts. When in 1924
the National Association of Real Estate Boards (NAREB)
adopted Article 34 of its professional Code of Ethics—"A Realtor should never be instrumental in introducing into a

neighborhood . . . members of a race or nationality, or any individuals whose presence will clearly be detrimental to property values in that neighborhood," it was merely codifying what had long been standard practice. (After the Supreme Court reversed itself in 1948 and made restrictive covenants unenforceable, NAREB changed its code to read, "A realtor should not be instrumental in introducing into a neighborhood a character of property or use which clearly will be detrimental to property values in that neighborhood.") If an American Dante should ever write an *Inferno* about race and ethnicity in America, surely a special place in hell would be reserved for many real estate agents.

African Americans in Chicago had begun to exercise political power in the World War I years. Republican Oscar De Priest was elected the city's first black alderman in 1915 and became the nation's first Northern black congressman in the following decade. The census of 1920 showed a black population in the city of 109,000, just over 4 percent of the city's more than 2.5 million persons. Thus at the time of the riot about 1 Chicagoan in 25 was an African American, whereas in 1910 the city's 44,000 blacks had been 1 Chicagoan in 50. Chicago was, in May 1919, "a city characterized by high social tensions," according to the sociologist Allan Grimshaw, tensions that continued throughout the immediate postwar period. In the two years before the riot, for example, "twenty-seven Negro dwellings" had been wrecked by bombs, and in the 20 months after the riots police records show 58 separate bomb explosions, almost all of them aimed at property rather than people and obviously in response to blacks moving into formerly all-white neighborhoods. The Chicago Commission on Race Relations (CCRR) later reported that "The collecting of arms by members of both races was known to the authorities, and it was evident that this was in preparation for aggression

as well as for self defense." (All subsequent quotations about
the Chicago riot are from this CCRR report.)

On June 21, 1919, two separate "wanton" murders of
African-American men occurred as they were returning
home through white neighborhoods. No one was arrested for
either crime, even after a white woman, who witnessed one of
the fatal attacks, pointed out the alleged murderer to a policeman. Shortly after the murders, notices were posted conspicu-
ously around the South Side warning that "We're going to get
the niggers on July 4th." There was no significant racial violence on that date, but twenty-three days later it erupted.

As has often been the case, an unforeseen incident provided
the spark that touched off the racial violence. The root causes
were clearly the racism that caused whites to fear and resent
the growth of the black population, and the increasing percep-
tion by blacks that even in the North they were not being
treated justly either by most of their fellow Chicagoans or by
the police and the justice system.

July 27, 1919, was a typically hot summer Sunday in
Chicago. Hundreds of whites and blacks crowded the beaches
at Twenty-sixth and Twenty-ninth streets, an area that then
marked the moving boundary between black and white
neighborhoods. Although there was no local ordinance stipu-
lating segregation of the beaches or anything else in Chicago,
what the CCRR called "an imaginary line in the water sepa-
rating the two beaches had been generally observed by the two
races." That Sunday, given the growing tensions, the line
served as a challenge rather than a barrier; stone-throwing incidents had involved groups of bathers who crossed it from either side. Finally Eugene Williams, a seventeen-year-old
African-American youth, entered the water from the beach
used by blacks, and drifted across the line to the white side
while holding on to a railroad tie. Spotted as an intruder, he

became the target of stones thrown by whites. He suddenly released the tie, slipped below the surface of Lake Michigan, and drowned. African Americans on the scene identified a young white named Stauber as the thrower of the "fatal stone," but a white policeman present on the beach refused to arrest the white youth. At that "crucial moment" he chose instead to arrest a black man on a white man's complaint. A group of blacks then attacked and beat the officer. The linked effects of these two events—the drowning of Eugene Williams and the refusal of the policeman to arrest his alleged killer—"marked the beginning of the riot," according to the CCRR report. (An all-white coroner's jury later found, officially, that Williams had drowned from fear of stone-throwing which kept him from the shore, and charged no person with a crime.)

Two hours later, at the scene of the drowning, a black man fired into a group of policemen and was killed by the return fire of a black officer. When crowds gathered near the beach, five white men were injured in a number of clashes. After dark, individual blacks were attacked in white neighborhoods. Between 9 p.m. and 3 a.m. at least twenty-seven blacks were beaten, seven stabbed, and four shot. Monday morning was quiet, and blacks went to work as usual, but on their return from work, many of those who had to pass through white neighborhoods were attacked. Streetcars were stopped and black passengers dragged into the street, beaten, stabbed, and shot. Blacks now began attacking whites, and by Tuesday morning the casualties from these clashes included four black men and five white men killed. Four blacks had also been killed by police.

At midnight Monday, because of a wage dispute unrelated to the riot, a strike interrupted streetcar and elevated train service. Thousands of black employees had to walk to work

Tuesday morning, and a number of them were killed while passing through white neighborhoods. White soldiers and sailors in uniform, along with some civilians, marauded through the downtown Loop area, killing two blacks and beating and robbing two others. Blacks living among white neighbors in Englewood, on the city's South Side and far from the major scenes of rioting, were driven from their homes, their household goods stolen, their houses burned and wrecked. What the CCRR called "an Italian mob," infuriated by a false rumor that an Italian-American girl had been shot by a black, killed the first black man it could get its hands on. Finally at 10:30 p.m. Wednesday the mayor reluctantly asked for National Guard troops which had been waiting since sometime Tuesday for such a call. That and rain Wednesday and Thursday brought the riot to an end by Friday, though on Saturday night, perhaps in retaliation, unknown persons set incendiary fires in white immigrant neighborhoods near the stockyards which destroyed 49 buildings and made 948 persons, mostly Lithuanian Americans, homeless.

For the entire riot period, July 27–31, the total known casualties were 38 dead—23 black and 15 white—and more than 500 injured, about two-thirds of them black. In contrast, two-thirds of the 229 persons arrested for riot activity were black, causing the Illinois state's attorney to charge that the Chicago police "were grossly unfair in making arrests." Indictments were even more lopsided: 17 blacks were indicted as opposed to 4 whites. Juries, however, generally failed to convict: only 3 blacks and 2 whites were found guilty of anything connected with the riot.

The Tulsa outrage, although essentially a "Southern style" riot, also had its "Northern" aspects as many blacks were armed and resisted. But once in full swing it was largely a one-way terrorization of the black community by invading armed whites. Tulsa was in some ways a typically medium-sized Southern city with racial segregation enforced by law, not by custom as in Chicago. The 1920 census found nearly 9,000 blacks in a population of 72,000, so that 1 Tulsan in 8 was black, most of them confined to menial occupations, though there was a small black middle class.

The proximate cause of the riot, too, was typically Southern. On May 31, 1921, a young black man, Dick Rowland, was accused of sexual assault—but not rape—against a young white elevator operator. Rowland was arrested and jailed at the county courthouse, and some in the black community feared he would be lynched. This was not an irrational assumption since at least sixty-four persons were lynched in the United States during 1921, fifty-nine of them blacks. In Tulsa itself the previous summer, a white man accused of murder had been taken from the jail by a mob of whites and lynched before an admiring crowd of two thousand.

Thus when word reached the black community on the evening of May 31, 1921, that armed whites had gathered at the courthouse, a group of fifty to seventy-five armed blacks arrived there at about 10:30 p.m. to offer their help in protecting the prisoner. The sheriff refused their help and asked them to leave, though he made no attempt to disperse the white crowd of fifteen hundred to two thousand, most of them armed. A single shot was fired, prompting a general fusillade. Walter White, who was later sent to Tulsa to investigate the riot for the NAACP, reported that a dozen persons fell as a result of these volleys.

From then until about 1 a.m., whites prepared for an invasion of the black quarter and some blacks prepared to defend themselves while others fled. Some whites broke into hardware and sporting goods stores to arm themselves, then began an all-out assault on the black district, firing indiscriminately, looting, and burning. Fires eventually destroyed about a square mile of the black district. The blacks' defense was hampered by their being vastly outnumbered and by the fact that local law enforcement officers, assisted by members of the Tulsa unit of the Oklahoma National Guard, were busy disarming and "interning" blacks but not whites. White mobs were so intent on destruction that the sheriff was able to spirit Dick Rowland safely out of town at about 8 a.m. the next morning. About an hour later a large contingent of Oklahoma guardsmen and its adjutant general arrived in Tulsa but did nothing until almost noon, when the governor was persuaded to declare martial law.

Once martial law had been declared, the guardsmen took charge of those blacks who had been interned and proceeded to round up others. On June 2 some four thousand blacks were confined, without being charged, at the local fairgrounds, under appalling conditions. The easiest way for a black person to get released was to have a white person, often an employer, vouch for him or her. All internees were released by June 15. Once released and for more than a month after the riot, blacks were required to carry an informal "passport" with the words "Police Protection" printed on one side and personal data on the other. While in custody, able-bodied black men and women "not having the care of children" were required to do uncompensated labor.

Since there was never an authoritative investigation of the Tulsa riot, no reliable casualty figures are available. Estimates range from 27 to more than 250 dead. The *New York Times*, for example, reported on the day after the riot that 9 whites and 68 blacks had been killed; six days later it reported only 33 deaths. Local sources have similar discrepancies. The leading historian of the riot, Scott Ellsworth, wrote in 1982 that "around seventy-five" deaths is probably the "most accurate" estimate. All the property damage was in the segregated area; in the aftermath of the riot, many blacks became refugees who fled the city and the state. Estimates of property damage also vary. One by the Tulsa Real Estate Exchange put real property destroyed at $1.5 million and personal property losses at half that amount. By June 2 relative calm returned to Tulsa.

The legal ramifications of the Tulsa riot could be termed farcical if they were not so tragic. An all-white grand jury of Tulsans, empaneled on June 9, issued its report on June 25. It was another case of "blaming the victim," strikingly similar to what the Springfield, Illinois, paper had written in 1908:

> ... The recent race riot was the direct result of an effort on the part of a certain group of colored men who appeared at the courthouse on the night of May 31, 1921 ... the [white] crowd assembled around the courthouse being purely spectators and curiosity seekers.... There was no mob spirit among the whites, no talk of lynching and no arms.

The jury's report went on to speak of

> indirect causes more vital to the public interest than the direct cause [including] certain propaganda and more or less agitation [that] had been going on among the colored population for some time [resulting] in the accumulation of firearms among the people and the storage of quantities of ammunition all of which was accumulative in the minds of the negro which led them as a people to believe in equal rights, social equality and their ability to demand the same.

The grand jury also issued indictments in twenty-seven cases, the most important of which charged fifty-seven persons, apparently all black men, with rioting. It was dismissed without a trial in November 1922, as were all the other cases, save two. The chief of police was first suspended and then convicted for misfeasance during the riot and for specific acts of corruption. One black Tulsan seems to have been sentenced to thirty days in the county jail for carrying a concealed weapon. As for the assault charge against Dick Rowland, the alleged victim refused to press charges, and he was eventually released.

No one has better expressed the rage felt by many African Americans during these tragic years than the Jamaica-born poet-novelist Claude McKay, who had immigrated to the United States early in the twentieth century and who became one of the leading figures of the Harlem Renaissance. His poem "If We Must Die," written in reaction to the "Red Summer," faces some of the grim realities of African-American life, though McKay himself never encountered extreme racist violence:

> If we must die, let it not be like hogs
> Hunted and penned in an inglorious spot,
> While round us bark the mad and hungry dogs,
> Making their mock at our accursed lot.
> If we must die, O let us nobly die,
> So that our precious blood may not be shed
> In vain; then even the monsters we defy
> Shall be constrained to honor us though dead!
> O kinsmen! We must meet the common foe!
> Though far outnumbered let us show us brave,
> And for their thousand blows deal one death blow!
> What though before us lies the open grave?
> Like men we'll face the murderous, cowardly pack
> Pressed to the wall, dying, but fighting back!

To be sure, most African Americans did not have to endure a race riot in these years. But there can have been few who did not feel some of the effects of the resurgence of racist violence in the postwar era, including violence from a revived and growing Ku Klux Klan. Still, the legal gradualism of the

NAACP was beginning to show results. In 1917 the Supreme Court, in one of the first decisions that marks the long and tortuous fifty-six-year retreat from *Plessy v. Ferguson,* declared legally mandated racial segregation in housing unconstitutional: it struck down Kentucky and Louisiana ordinances requiring that blacks and whites live on separate city blocks. More significant, however, in the same year the Court upheld restrictive covenants. In other words, the Court held that while public action creating residential segregation was illegal, private agreements that created segregation could be enforced by public bodies. Thus, in years to come, massive segregated housing proliferated in Northern cities and, beginning in the 1930s, the federal government built separate segregated housing projects for each race.

In the face of these events, many African Americans turned to a kind of chauvinistic nationalism, not very different from that espoused in these years by many whites. The key black nationalist leader in the war and postwar years was Marcus Garvey, an unnaturalized immigrant from Jamaica who was a truly charismatic figure. In 1914 he founded the Universal Negro Improvement Association (UNIA) and two years later began organizing in New York. The UNIA quickly—and briefly—became the largest African-American organization of any kind, enrolling hundreds of thousands if not millions of blacks. It had the sympathy of many more. The historian J. Saunders Redding remembered, three decades later, a UNIA meeting in his hometown, Wilmington, Delaware. His description illustrates that, in techniques, the UNIA resembled religious revival meetings.

> [The UNIA members] came with much shouting and blare of bugles and a forest of flags—a black star centered in a red field.... Young women ... in the uniforms distributed millions of streamers bearing the slogan "Back to Africa."

[The UNIA members] were not people of the slums, they
were men with small struggling shops and restaurants, and
personal servants. . . .

While the UNIA established chapters across the country,
Garvey's headquarters was in New York City's Harlem,
where he was but one element in the vibrant culture created
there, a culture nowhere better depicted than in Ralph Elli-
son's superb novel *The Invisible Man* (1945).

Garvey espoused a variety of black nationalism that mirrored but reversed the views of most whites. Where the latter
believed that blacks were inferior (a distinguished white
American paleontologist, Henry Fairfield Osborn, could
write in a learned journal in 1926 that the intelligence of Negroes rarely exceeded "that of the eleven-year-old youth of the
species *Homo sapiens*"), Garvey increasingly emphasized a
theme of racial separation and purity. He told blacks to reject intermarriage and social equality and declared himself
in favor of a "pure black race just as self-respecting whites are
in favor of [a] pure white race." He accompanied this by attacking black leaders of mixed ancestry as "mongrels" and
"miscegenationists." One such black leader, W. E. B. Du Bois,
argued that Garvey was either a "lunatic or a traitor"; Garvey
insisted that the NAACP leader was simply "a white man's
nigger."

The most publicized aspect of Garvey's UNIA was its impossible project of "returning" all ten million black Americans
to Africa. For this purpose Garvey created, mostly on paper, a
Black Star Steamship Company and collected relatively large
amounts of money from his devoted followers. Whatever else
he was, Garvey was a disastrous businessman, and in 1923 the
steamship "line" was declared bankrupt. Garvey himself was
tried, convicted of fraud, jailed, and then deported, but his fol-

lowers and adherents, then and now, are convinced he was framed by federal agents.

If black Americans focused on the "Red Summer" of 1919—red for the African-American blood that was shed—many white Americans, especially middle-class whites, were caught up in the "Red Scare" of 1919–1920—red for communism, socialism, or any kind of radicalism. During the war many American socialists, native and foreign-born, had opposed on principle American entry into a "capitalist war." The federal government and many, perhaps most, Americans had translated this opposition into pro-German and thus "un-American" sentiments. The wartime Espionage and Sedition Acts, as noted, had been used to persecute American radicals, often on the flimsiest excuses. The Sedition Act made public antiwar statements a crime. Eugene Victor Debs, who had received almost a million votes for president in 1912—almost 6 percent of those cast—was indicted, tried, convicted, and sent to federal prison for sedition. In his case, it consisted of making a speech in which he said, "The master class has always declared the wars; the subject class has always fought the battles. The master class has had all to gain and nothing to lose, while the subject class has had nothing to gain and all to lose—especially their lives." These words would, according to the indictment, interfere with recruiting for the armed forces, one of the offenses specified in the wartime law.

This kind of hysterical overreaction by the federal government did not end with the armistice; in fact, only after the war did American antiradicalism reach its early-twentieth-century crescendo in what one liberal official, Assistant Secretary of Labor Louis F. Post, later called a "deportation delirium." Most of the fears about the dangers that domestic radicals posed to the United States were groundless. Both of the

American Communist parties were, in terms of electoral politics, impotent; the Socialist party had been crippled both by
government persecution and by internal divisions over the nature of Soviet bolshevism; the Industrial Workers of the
World had been all but destroyed; and the trade union movement, hardly radical by most standards, was in decline after its
Progressive Era–World War I growth. To be sure, there were
some large strikes, particularly in 1919, most notably a massive work stoppage in the steel industry and the first general
strike in American history in Seattle, both of which were essentially peaceful. There were also a number of terrorist bomb
outrages, presumably committed by radicals. The most deadly
was an explosion set off during the noon hour on Wall Street
in September 1919, killing thirty-eight persons and wounding
hundreds more. Because many of the postwar radicals and
perhaps most of the few thousand in Communist parties were
foreign-born, the press was able to imprint the image of the
bearded, bomb-throwing foreign radical almost indelibly on
the American mind.

Wilson's postwar attorney general, A. Mitchell Palmer, a
liberal urban Northern Democrat with presidential ambi-
tions, instituted the first nationwide hunt for subversives. He
was aided by a young Justice Department clerk, J. Edgar
Hoover, who later as director of the Federal Bureau of Investigation would dominate "red hunting" for almost fifty years.
Thousands of radicals, real and imagined, were arrested in
1920 by federal agents from Boston to Seattle, often without
even the hint of probable cause, and hundreds were deported
in hurried procedures which ignored due process of law. Most
notorious was the exile of 249 radicals to the Soviet Union on a
vessel called the *Buford*, quickly dubbed by the press the "Soviet Ark." Among those deported was the anarchist feminist
Emma Goldman, who had lived in the United States since

1885, when she was sixteen years old, and who is now regarded as one of the more influential American women of the twentieth century.

These federal activities were mirrored in most states, and state law enforcement officers often paid even less attention to civil liberties than their federal counterparts. A number of states passed laws directed at radicals, often under the rubric of "criminal syndicalism." Following the wartime federal example set by the Sedition Act and exemplified by the Debs case, these mostly postwar laws made it a crime to advocate violence or something that might lead to violence. In one extreme instance, a young woman in California was indicted and convicted of criminal syndicalism for hoisting a red flag—symbol of revolution—on a flagpole at a camp for young people sponsored by a radical organization. The Supreme Court eventually threw out this conviction, but many others sentenced under state syndicalism laws had to serve their terms.

The case that came to exemplify the antiradical, antiforeign prejudices of America and most Americans in the 1920s— called by some the "case that would not die"—involved the conviction and eventual electrocution of two Italian immigrant anarchists, Nicola Sacco and Bartolomeo Vanzetti. They were arrested, tried, and convicted in 1921 for participation in a payroll robbery in South Braintree, Massachusetts, in which a guard was shot and killed. The evidence against them was, to say the least, dubious. Even a casual perusal of the printed record of their trial reveals that, by the standards of the time, they did not get a fair trial. They were convicted not because of the evidence but because they were Italians, anarchists, and had fled to Mexico during the war to avoid possible military service. One reputable individual even swore that the judge had said, in the presumed privacy of a golf club's locker room,

that he would "get those Wop bastards." The case became a
cause célèbre, not only for radicals but for such modern liber-
als as Harvard law professor Felix Frankfurter, who wrote a
devastating critique of the way the case was handled. It is
probably more than coincidental that Frankfurter, who later
became a Supreme Court justice, was a Jew born in Vienna
and that the presiding judge he criticized, Webster Thayer,
was a Boston Brahmin descended from colonial forebears.

After the death sentence had been pronounced, the case became the focus of the first worldwide civil liberties protest.
Even the pope joined in vain appeals for clemency. Sacco and
Vanzetti were electrocuted in 1927. Some revisionist historians have attempted to "prove" the guilt or innocence of one or
both of the victims, but that is beside the point. Under the
American system of justice it is the function of juries, not historians, to decide guilt or innocence. The role of the historian
is to judge whether or not the trial was fair, and, if unfair, why
that was so. By that standard it is clear that Sacco and Vanzetti
were convicted not on the evidence but because of who they
were and the way in which the prosecution and the judge allowed that to influence the jury. Whatever we may think of
this trial and the entire "Red Scare," we must understand that
they were both highly popular with the general public, which
probably would have welcomed similar disposition of many
other immigrant radicals.

Most foreign-born Americans and the immigrant and ethnic communities they lived in were not directly affected by the
postwar crusade against radicals and foreigners. Typically the
people of those communities, like most other Americans, were
trying to reorient their lives to the changed postwar situation.
For many, particularly recent immigrants from Europe, there
were transatlantic ties to be reestablished, visits to be made,
and, in some cases, family migrations to be completed. For

Mexican-American families, such reunifications now became more difficult. Many Mexicans had practiced a circular migration, in which individuals and whole families might go back and forth across the border over a considerable period of time. During the war years, as we have seen, the federal government facilitated such movements by issuing temporary visas to persons thought to be temporary workers. By 1921 that policy had changed, and the old regulations about visa requirements, plus some new ones, were enforced. This made much circular migration impossible to conduct legally and the rest more expensive, difficult, and time consuming. As the historian George J. Sánchez has noted, Mexicans "who had grown accustomed to legal, relatively easy passage across the border were now faced with the prospect of venturing north illegally or being held up in border cities indefinitely."

But for many leaders of European immigrant and ethnic communities who were concerned with home-country politics, the postwar period was a time of opportunity, a time when they could lobby to obtain more favorable treatment for their motherlands at the peace table and later. This was not a new development: ethnic communities in the United States had long tried to get the federal government to take action benefiting their fellows still abroad. No group had—or has— played this role more effectively than American Jews, who as early as 1840 petitioned President Martin Van Buren to protest the mistreatment of Jews in the Ottoman Empire. Before, during, and after the Versailles Conference, the minority of American Jews who were Zionists lobbied intensively for President Wilson and his successors to pressure the British to respect the wartime Balfour Declaration, which promised a "Jewish homeland" in what was then Palestine.

Although the situation of American Jews was unique, similar lobbying had long been carried on by other groups, partic-

ularly Irish Americans and Polish Americans seeking independence for their countries of origin. Some Polish-American
leaders had long talked of American Polonia as "the fifth
province of Poland." Since many of Woodrow Wilson's Fourteen Points called for "self-determination" for subject peoples
in Europe, his trips to the peace conference, the ensuing debate over the peace treaty, and the presidential election of 1920
all provided what many ethnic leaders in America saw as
golden opportunities to make their influence—and votes—in
the New World affect the rearrangement of the Old. Not only
Polish, Irish, and Jewish leaders but representatives of Greeks,
Italians, Czechs, Slovaks, and a number of other ethnic groups
lobbied the government and politicians in and out of office.
Often these leaders were at odds. For example, while all
Greek-American leaders wanted Greek interests supported
vis-à-vis those of Turkey, some worked for a republican form
of government, others for a monarchy. The results of these
various attempts to influence American policy were at best
mixed, but it is clear they provided nativists with even more
"evidence" that immigrants—or most of them—were "un-
Americans" who cared more about their homeland than their
adopted country.

The anti-immigrant mood continued in Congress. Picking
up where they had left off in 1917, nativist legislators resumed
their attempts to curtail immigration drastically when the
lame-duck Congress met in December 1920. In the more
volatile House of Representatives, a bill was introduced, debated, and passed, without any of the customary hearings, in
one week. By a vote of 296 to 42, an absolute majority of both
parties, the House proposed to halt all immigration for one
year, making it the most severe immigration bill ever acted on
favorably by either chamber, before or since. The more conservative Senate shelved the bill and substituted a quota mea-

sure introduced by William P. Dillingham, who had headed the U.S. Immigration Commission before the war. The House agreed, somewhat reluctantly, and after the conferees had lowered the number of immigrants to be admitted, a bill was sent to the White House just days before Woodrow Wilson left office. In one of his last acts, Wilson used the pocket veto, since a vote to override would surely have followed a regular veto.

This setback to nativist hopes would not last long. The new Republican president had run on a platform that warned against permitting too many immigrants to enter the country and went on to call for "higher standards" of admission and to "favor immigrants whose standards are similar to ours." It also argued that "all aliens should be required to register annually" and that "no alien should become a citizen until he has become genuinely American." No one doubted that Warren Harding would honor that pledge.

5

The Triumph of Nativism

NO DECADE in American history has been so variously described by historians as the 1920s. The earliest interpretations, of which the journalist Frederick Lewis Allen's *Only Yesterday* (1931) is the most enduring, stressed the colorful and anecdotal aspects of the so-called Jazz Age. Later, political historians used the decade as a foil for Franklin Roosevelt's New Deal which succeeded it; here the exemplar is Arthur M. Schlesinger's *The Crisis of the Old Order* (1960). Similarly, economic historians saw the "prosperity decade" and the "depression decade" as almost polar opposites. More recently, economic historians such as Ellis Hawley, stressing an organizational interpretation, have seen the period as a "search for modern order." Hawley has argued that the period from 1922 through 1928, "long depicted as the Indian Summer of an outdated and passing economic order, really stands as a kind of premature spring for the capitalist adaptations of our own time." Cultural historians, such as Lynn Dumenil, have seen modernity as a key element in describing the twenties.

All these interpretations, except the first, have some validity, but for the purposes of this book I prefer to treat the period—or more particularly its first half—as a time of social disorganization and conflict, when contending groups of Americans struggled to maintain their dominance or to win a place in the sun. John Higham's wonderful phrase, the "tribal twenties," strikes just the right note. If we think of the main tribes as teams, we can speak of four different contests going on simultaneously: rural versus urban, dry versus wet, Protestant versus Catholic, and native stock versus immigrant stock. Many Americans played in all four contests. To them the issues involved seemed monumental and permanent. We now know that these issues would soon be dwarfed by the economic concerns of the Great Depression. By 1936 a majority of each of the eight tribes listed above could take part, along with others, in the Roosevelt coalition, led by an urban wet Protestant who managed to appeal strongly to most members of all the other groups.

As the Census of 1890 had announced the end of the frontier, that of 1920 announced the existence, for the first time, of an urban majority. The United States, as Richard Hofstader liked to point out, was born in the country and only later moved to town. The first census in 1790 had shown that just 5 percent of the people lived in any kind of urban area; by 1920 slightly over half the people lived in such areas and 26 percent lived in cities of more than 100,000 population. Large numbers of this urban majority were not Protestants, were of immigrant stock, and were largely wet, that is, opposed to Prohibition. The larger the city, the more this tended to be the case, with strongly Protestant, old-stock Los Angeles the major exception.

The twenties began with the election of Republican Warren G. Harding by a landslide, more than 60 percent of the popular vote. His victory meant both the rejection of Woodrow Wilson and the end of the Progressive Era. While in most histories this change of both party and orientation seems drastic, from the point of view of the minority groups who form the focus of this book, it seemed to make little difference. An absolute majority of Americans of both parties showed little concern for the condition of American Indians, heartily endorsed segregation, and favored immigration restriction. The relatively few African Americans who were eligible voters voted overwhelmingly for Republicans who, historically, had tended to be less overtly hostile to the aspirations of black people than were the Democrats.

American Indians benefited from the Indian Citizenship Act, passed by Congress in 1924, which for the first time made all American Indians citizens of the United States. This was not an unmixed blessing, as many Western politicians tried with some success to use the Indians' new citizen status as an excuse for eliminating even further those special protections that still existed for Indian property and tribal rights. (Later, in the 1940s, citizenship made all Indian men eligible for the military draft, while in the Eisenhower years some politicians, such as Utah Senator Arthur V. Watkins, argued that citizenship automatically extinguished all Indian treaty rights, a specious contention which happily found little support in Congress and none in the courts.)

Western politicians meanwhile continued their assault on Indian property rights. The elevation, in 1921, of New Mexico's Republican Senator Albert B. Fall to Harding's cabinet as secretary of the interior, the officer in charge of Indian policy, augured no good for the Indian people. Fall, now notorious as a cabinet-level thief who later went to jail for his role in transferring government oil lands to a private businessman, should also be infamous for his long-standing efforts to transfer Indian property rights to whites, including members of his own family. Not Fall himself but his daughter-in-law, son-in-law, and ranch manager all were able to obtain favorable leases on land belonging to the Mescalero Apaches while Fall was a major force in Indian affairs in Washington. Even by 1920s standards, when notions of conflict of interest were much less developed than in post-Watergate America, Fall's actions with regard to American Indians regularly crossed the line of what was permissible. One of his attempts to despoil Indians was so blatant that a new and eventually powerful Indian reform movement was created to block it.

The attempt in question was a bill introduced by Republican Senator Holm O. Bursum of New Mexico at the request of Interior Secretary Fall. It was an attempt to settle long-standing disputes between Pueblo Indians and non-Indians over land titles and water rights in the Rio Grande Valley, some of them stretching back to the Treaty of Guadelupe Hidalgo of 1848, which ended the Mexican War. As one might expect from a bill emanating from Fall, it was strongly biased against Indians and favored white claimants. Two separate versions of the bill had passed the Senate before significant opposition developed. Stella Atwood of Riverside, California, a leader of the General Federation of Women's Clubs and a longtime supporter of Indian causes, spearheaded the anti–Bursum Bill forces. She not only protested vigorously but also interested John Collier in Indian reform and secured financing for him to investigate government Indian policy under the auspices of her women's organization.

Collier's chief interest had been in the Americanization of immigrants. Unlike most Americanizers of the era, however, he stressed a pluralistic point of view which emphasized immigrant cultural values as well as those of their adopted country. Accordingly, Collier rejected the assimilationist position which held that the Indian's only hope was to emulate the white man; instead he stressed Indian cultural values. Thus he not only mobilized white opposition to the Bursum bills and their successors, he also encouraged Indians to organize and protest. In part due to his activities, 121 representatives from twenty Pueblos met in November 1922—Collier later claimed it was the first confederation of the Pueblo Indians since their revolt against the Spanish in 1680—and adopted a protest to be sent to Congress. Collier, who had a genius for publicity appropriate in what some have called an age of ballyhoo, saw that it was printed in the *New York Times*. When he later escorted a delegation of New Mexico Indians to Washington to testify before the Senate, he arranged for what we would today call photo opportunities in Chicago and New York, including ceremonial singing and dancing at the New York Stock Exchange. The Bursum Bill never became law as Idaho's progressive Republican Senator William E. Borah, a Collier ally, arranged to have it buried in a Senate committee. More important, major Indian reforms proposed by Collier and others drew much attention. Collier himself, the outsider in the twenties, would become commissioner of Indian affairs in 1933 and administer the "Indian New Deal" for the next dozen years.

Despite these positive developments, the twenties saw very little change for the vast majority of American Indians. They were still the poorest group in American society, with the lowest income, fewest material goods, highest infant mortality rates, and shortest life spans. By the end of the twenties it could be argued that Helen Hunt Jackson's "century of dishonor" had become a century and a half.

For most African Americans, the 1920s marked a continued recession from the high hopes of the early war months. During the twenties the net migration of blacks from South to North reached 750,000, surpassing the number who had moved during the great migration of the World War I years. Still, the South remained home to 79 percent of African Americans according to the 1930 census. Large Northern cities, particularly New York and Chicago, received almost all these migrants who, with the growing numbers of Northern-born blacks, made up an increasing but still small percentage of their population. Only in Chicago did black Americans have more than token political representation.

On the national political scene, the only initiative close to a civil rights measure was a campaign to make lynching a federal crime. Because local prosecutors had failed to indict and local juries to convict, all but a handful of lynchers had gone unpunished. In 1921, a year in which at least fifty-nine blacks were lynched, Representative Leonidas C. Dyer, a Missouri Republican, introduced an antilynching bill which passed the House by a vote of 230 to 119. But the expected filibuster by Southerners prevented it from being voted on in the Senate. Even without a bill, lynching was in decline in the 1920s, but at least 281 African Americans were nonetheless murdered in that manner, more than a lynching every other week. (In the 1890s the figure had been 1,026, about two such killings every week.)

Perhaps nothing better exemplifies the disdain with which most of the American establishment held African Americans than the following report on "Negro Manpower" issued by the U.S. Army War College in 1925:

> In the process of evolution the American negro has not pro-gressed as far as other sub species of the human family. . . .
> The cranial capacity of the negro is smaller than whites.
> . . . The psychology of the negro, based on heredity derived from mediocre African ancestors, cultivated by generations of slavery, is one from which we cannot expect to draw leadership material. . . . In general the negro is jolly, docile, tractable, and lively but with harsh or unkind treatment can become stubborn, sullen and unruly. In physical

courage [he] falls well back of whites. . . . He is most sus-
ceptible to "Crowd Psychology." He cannot control himself
in fear of danger. . . . He is a rank coward in the dark.

Note that this appraisal fits both the stereotype imprinted by
The Birth of a Nation and other racist propaganda and the notions of "scientific racism."

No examination of black America during the 1920s would
be complete without a look at the Harlem Renaissance, an ex-
traordinary flowering of African-American literary culture
which was centered in that section of Manhattan. Harlem had
been a Jewish neighborhood earlier in the century. Its evolution into America's most famous black neighborhood is a classic example of what urban geographers call "migrant
succession," in which later migrant groups succeeded earlier
ones. Important figures in the Harlem Renaissance included,
in addition to the poet Claude McKay, the journalist and author Langston Hughes, the anthropologist and author Zora
Neale Hurston, and the poet Countee Cullen. Collectively the
work that came out of the Renaissance drew attention not
only to its creators but also to the facts of African-American
life. It caused some white American literary figures to exam-
ine seriously the condition of black Americans. Eugene
O'Neill's play about racial intermarriage, *All God's Chillun Got
Wings* (1924), is perhaps the most important example of this
fleeting phenomenon.

But the luster and prestige of the Harlem Renaissance
made little difference in the lives of most African Americans,
who continued to live as second-class citizens in both South
and North. They experienced in the 1920s new onslaughts
from a reborn Ku Klux Klan, chartered in Atlanta at the end
of 1916. Unlike the original Klan of the Reconstruction era,
the new KKK quickly spread out of the South and attacked

not only blacks but Catholics, Jews, and immigrants. By the mid-1920s, when its influence was at its peak, it had perhaps five million members. Nowhere was it stronger than in Indiana and Oregon where Klan-backed politicians became dominant. Using slogans such as "America for Americans," "Militant Protestanism," and "White Supremacy," the Klan insisted that "human liberty is possible ONLY under Protestant Christianity."

Although the second Klan was clearly a hate organization, Klan members saw themselves as the defenders of an older American order threatened by foreigners, foreign religions, foreign cultures, and by modernism itself. Klansmen and women saw themselves as defenders of family values. Dr. A. H. Hughes, editor of the Klan newspaper in Phoenix, Arizona, attacked Catholics, Jews, Mormons, and Negroes, in that order. He claimed that:

> Every criminal, every gambler, every thug, every libertine, every girl-runner, every home-wrecker, every wife-beater, every dope peddler, every moonshiner, every crooked politician, every pagan papal priest, every shyster, every K[night] of C[olumbus], every white slaver, every brothel madam, every Roman controlled newspaper is fighting against the Ku Klux Klan. THINK IT OVER. WHICH SIDE ARE YOU ON? GET OFF THE FENCE!

While some of the Klan's political influence came from officials who shared its views, perhaps equally important were those politicians who feared defeat by the potent "Klan vote." Many, like Hugo Black of Alabama, later an important liberal senator and Supreme Court justice, joined the Klan for the same reason they joined fraternal orders—to get votes— without really believing in what the Klan stood for. Some business persons joined the Klan for presumed economic advantage: many establishments in areas of Klan strength displayed the acronym TWK—meaning "trade with a Klansman"—in their windows or advertisements. Other joiners fully shared the Klan's bigotry. In some parts of the country the Klan was well represented in the trade union movement. Perhaps the best indication of its strength in the mid-1920s was the refusal of a bare majority of the delegates to the 1924 Democratic National Convention to support a resolution condemning the Klan. It was defeated by one vote out of 1,083. The following year 40,000 Klansmen in full regalia marched through the streets of the nation's capital.

Scandals involving vicious crimes by Klan politicians in Indiana and elsewhere, plus exposures of the moneymaking side of the Klan operation (a few organizers received a goodly percentage of the $10 initiation fee each member was supposed to pay), caused the Klan's political clout to disappear almost overnight as the organization all but collapsed in the later 1920s. But the attitudes and fears of social change which the Klan and other hate groups exploited had deep roots among a large part of the American population.

One person who was able to exploit those fears, at least for a time, was the auto magnate Henry Ford, who spent millions of his own dollars disseminating the vilest sort of anti-Jewish propaganda in his newspaper, the *Dearborn Independent*. Ford, who had little formal education, believed all kinds of nonsense, much of which was harmless: history was "bunk"; sugar should be avoided because the sharp edges of its crystals would damage one's insides; the ability of some chickens to avoid being run over by automobiles "proved" they had been run over in a previous incarnation and had learned from it. But he also believed that Jews had a gigantic and diabolical plot to run the world for their own benefit. He reprinted and distributed a crude nineteenth-century tsarist Russian forgery, usually called the *Protocols of the Elders of Zion*, which purported to be the minutes of the Elders of Zion, an imaginary secret international Jewish organization in control of the world and responsible for most of its evils, including World War I, poverty, and so forth. Successful lawsuits caused him publicly to recant these views in 1927 and to cease propagating them.

Anti-Semitism in the 1920s was not only the preserve of the undereducated. In 1922 the president of Harvard University, A. Lawrence Lowell, announced that henceforth Harvard would have a quota for Jews. This was not, like recent affirmative-action quotas (usually described as goals), a device to get more Jews into Harvard but a way to reduce their numbers. Lowell was simply doing openly what many elite private universities had been doing secretly for some time, and would continue to do until after World War II. The reason was that Jewish students then, as with some Asian-American students now, were "overrepresented" in these institutions—more of them were admitted in competitive examinations than their incidence in the population would suggest. (Jews were perhaps 3 percent of the population.) Anti-Semitism was thoroughly entrenched at every level of American society: many companies would not knowingly hire Jews, many resort hotels would not allow Jews as guests, many apartment houses would not rent to them.

The much larger Catholic minority faced similar hostility and discrimination. Many Americans sincerely believed the Catholic church was a menace to American democracy, and that Catholics buried a rifle under the local church altar for every Catholic boy born, part of a long-standing conspiracy which some day would seek to overthrow the Republic. Controversies over Catholic New York politician Alfred E. Smith's quest for the Democratic presidential nomination, and then for the presidency, were only the tip of the iceberg of anti-Catholic prejudice. One major difference between these two religious prejudices is that while anti-Catholicism was prevalent only among Protestants, anti-Semitism prevailed among all Christians. The most important purveyor of anti-Semitism in the United States in the 1930s was the Canadian-born Catholic priest Charles E. Coughlin.

When President Harding called the newly elected Congress into special session in March 1921, the question of immigration "reform" was high on the agenda. Given the record of the previous Congress, when only Wilson's pocket veto had prevented the passage of highly restrictive legislation, the question was not whether an anti-immigrant bill would pass but what kind of bill it would be. There were still those in Congress who wished to halt all immigration, at least temporarily.

By May 1921 the new Congress had reenacted, without serious debate, the bill that Wilson had vetoed. It passed the Senate by a vote of 78 to 1 and the House without a recorded vote, and Harding quickly signed it into law. Since this law initiated a quota system which in one form or another was the ruling principle of American immigration legislation for forty-four years, it is important to understand its origins and provisions.

As noted earlier, in 1911 the U.S. Immigration Commission, using the word "race" to mean "nationality," had recommended that "the limitation of each [race] arriving each year be limited to a certain percentage of that race arriving during a given period of years." The chairperson of that commission, William P. Dillingham, a moderate restrictionist, was still in the Senate in 1920–1921, and his views prevailed over those of the extreme restrictionists led by Representative Albert Johnson, chair of the House Immigration Committee. Johnson, unlike Dillingham, was a blatant anti-Semite who secured access to reports from like-minded American consuls in Europe and used statements from them to argue that the United States was in danger of being overrun by hordes of "abnormally twisted" and "unassimilable" Jews, "filthy, un-American and often dangerous in their habits." In the preceding Congress, Johnson's committee had brought in a bill halting all immigration for two years; the full House had cut it to one year, anticipating that Congress would work out a totally new system during the pause. Not even the extreme restrictionists believed that all immigration should be stopped indefinitely.

The Senate substituted a bill drafted principally by Dillingham. While its major thrust was to reduce the flow of immigrants from eastern and southern Europe—primarily Italians, Poles, Jews, southern Slavs, and Greeks, very few of whom were Protestants—it had many provisions that were fair and equitable. It would not apply to immigration from the Western Hemisphere—Canadians, Mexicans, and others could come and go as before; and it left alone the existing arrangements for Asian immigration. Thus the exemptions for Chinese "treaty merchants" and their families remained in effect, and the Gentlemen's Agreement still governed immigration from Japan, while most other Asians continued to be kept out by the existing "barred zone." For Europeans there were numerical limits—quotas—which would allow the yearly migration of a maximum of 5 percent of the number of foreign-born from each country already in the United States according to data from the 1910 census (the latest figures then available). Dillingham's bill, also a one-year "emergency" measure, would permit a maximum of 600,000 quota immigrants each year, but it was assumed that many of the quota spaces from some nations, such as Great Britain, would be un-used. Such unused spaces could *not* be used by persons from countries whose quotas were filled.

The more extreme House of Representatives reluctantly ac-cepted the quota principle and other provisions of the Senate bill. But it lowered the annual percentage admissible from each eligible nation from 5 to 3 percent, reducing the maxi-mum number of annual quota spaces to some 350,000. Aliens under the age of eighteen who were children of United States citizens were exempt from quota limitation, and other close relatives of citizens or resident aliens who had filed for citi-zenship papers received preference within the quotas. There were other minor exemptions. Termed the Emergency Quota Act of 1921, this law marked the first time a numerical cap had been placed on immigration and represents a pivotal point in the history of American immigration policy. But since it exempted the Western Hemisphere from quotas, the law did not attempt fully to control immigration. Writing a "per-manent bill" proved more complicated than congressional leaders had anticipated, and just as the one-year measure was about to expire in May 1922, Congress extended it for two more years, setting the stage for a major immigration debate in 1924.

That debate, like the more limited discussions in 1921, was not about whether immigration should be restricted but about how it should be restricted. The 1924 debate centered on four major issues. First, should the quota system be based on the now available 1920 census, as Dillingham intended; second, should the New World remain outside the quota system; third, should the special arrangement on Japanese immigra-tion, the Gentlemen's Agreement, be allowed to stand; and fourth, what kind of "permanent" system of immigration con-trol should be established.

Moderate restrictionists wanted to make the 1921 law permanent, to base the quotas on the latest available census, to keep the Western Hemisphere quota-free, and either to continue the Gentlemen's Agreement or to give Japan a quota. Extreme restrictionists wanted a nonvariable and smaller quota which would reduce immigration, extend the quota to the New World, and bar Japanese along with other Asians. The extremists, as we shall see, won the first and third arguments but lost the second. Other issues, some of them quite significant, were largely ignored in the congressional debates. As would often be the case with immigration legislation, Congress did not fully understand the implications of the legislation it passed. The history of immigration legislation is filled with unintended consequences.

The new law pushed the base line of the quota system back to the 1890 census and lowered the percentage from 3 to 2 percent. The reasons for this were frankly stated: from the restrictionists' point of view, the existing law was allowing in too many of the wrong kinds of people—non-Protestant eastern and southern Europeans. Updating to the 1920 census would have allowed in even more. The leader of the extreme restrictionist forces in the House, Albert Johnson, calculated that instead of the 42,000 Italian and 31,000 Polish annual quota spaces crated by using a 2 percent quota based on the 1920 census, a similar quota based on the 1890 census would cut the numbers to 4,000 Italians and 6,000 Poles. In terms of total numbers, 2 percent of the 1920 foreign-born white population would have produced an annual quota of some 270,000; the adopted 1890 base provided only 180,000 quota spaces, a far cry from Dillingham's original 600,000.

But the restrictionists were unable to place a numerical limitation on Western Hemisphere immigration, partly because many Southwestern and Western legislators insisted that their regions needed Mexican agricultural labor. Congress did, however, narrow the Western Hemisphere exemption. Where the 1921 law had exempted from quota limitation anyone who had lived for five years in the hemisphere, the 1924 law exempted only persons born in its independent nations, plus Canada, Newfoundland, and the Canal Zone. Persons born in other New World European colonies were admissible as quota immigrants charged to the quota of the mother country. Those removed from the quota-free category were almost all blacks from the Caribbean.

The Senate seemed ready to insist on a special arrangement for the Japanese, chiefly because of Japan's economic and military importance. Moderates argued that either the Gentlemen's Agreement be continued or Japan be given a quota. Under the Gentlemen's Agreement an average of some 7,700 Japanese, mostly women, had been entering annually since 1920, while under the 2 percent/1890 formula Japan would have been entitled to a quota of 100 annually. But Senator Henry Cabot Lodge stampeded the Senate into believing that a phrase in a letter from the Japanese ambassador had threatened the United States, and the proud Japanese were shut out under the formula that no "alien ineligible to citizenship" could enter the United States as an immigrant. It was safe to use this formula, for the Supreme Court in the 1922 case of *Ozawa v. U.S.* had ruled that the 1870 statute restricting naturalization to "white persons and persons of African descent" was constitutional and that Japanese were not "white persons."

In addition to the Western Hemisphere natives noted above, nonquota immigrants in the 1924 law included wives and unmarried children of U.S. citizens under eighteen years of age (husbands of U.S. citizens were added only in 1928, and then only if the marriage had taken place before June 1, 1928);

previously admitted immigrants returning from a visit
abroad; any minister of any religious denomination or professor of a college, academy, seminary, or university and his wife
(but not husband) and unmarried children under eighteen;
and women who had previously lost their citizenship by marriage or from the loss of citizenship by their husbands. Bona
fide students were admissible, and the long-established rights
of Chinese "treaty merchants" and their families to domicile
within the United States were reaffirmed.

The provision for women was an indirect result of the 1920
woman suffrage amendment. In 1922 the Cable Act ended the
automatic granting or revocation of citizenship to married
women solely because of the status of their husbands. Before
1922 an alien woman who married a citizen or whose husband
became naturalized automatically became an American citizen. Conversely, any female citizen, native born or naturalized, who married an alien, was divested of her citizenship.
Both automatic granting and divestment of citizenship ended
as Congress declared that "the right of any woman to become
a naturalized citizen of the United States shall not be denied
or abridged because of her sex or because she is a married
woman." But there was a joker for a few women: the law also
provided that "any woman citizen who marries an alien ineligible to citizenship"—in other words, an Asian of any nationality—"shall cease to be a citizen of the United States." Men's
marriages were not affected either before or after 1922. No
man ever gained or lost citizenship because of marriage.

For the first time visas were required of all immigrants,
which directly involved the consular service of the Department of State in the regulation of immigration. A nine-dollar
charge for visas, added to the eight-dollar head tax, meant an
outlay of seventeen dollars to enter the United States. While
this sum was hardly a major deterrent to immigrants who

were paying for an Atlantic passage, it was significant to Mexican immigrants, who were long used to crossing and recross-
ing the border casually. The act also required reentry permits
for aliens leaving the country and wishing to return, at three
dollars for each crossing, which also encouraged Mexicans to
come and go "informally." As George Sánchez explains,
"Workers who had grown accustomed to legal, relatively easy
passage across the border were now faced with the prospect of
venturing north illegally or being held up in border cities indefinitely."

The statutory requirement of a visa, which had to be ob-
tained at an American consulate, was thought to be most important by restrictionists. It was, in their terminology, a way of
controlling immigration at the source, and it gave considerable discretionary authority to individual consular officials.
Their rulings were almost never subject to review unless the
prospective immigrants could call on someone in the United
States who was interested in their admission. No thorough
study exists of how the consular service regulated the issuance
of visas, but it is quite clear that officials such as Wilbur J.
Carr, who directed the consular service from 1909 to 1937,
viewed their roles as gatekeepers, and that Carr and many of
his subordinates were nativists. Carr, for example, had egged
Representative Johnson on by sending him a stream of letters
filled with warnings about immigrants. One of them described "the great mass of aliens passing through Rotterdam"
as "Russian Poles or Polish Jews of the usual ghetto
type ... every possible care and safeguard should be used to
keep out [such] undesirables."

Nativists of all sorts rejoiced at the passage of the 1924 act.
Whatever we may think of it today, the act probably reflected
the desires of most Americans accurately. Both major parties
supported it, as did the American trade union movement.

President Calvin Coolidge, who signed the act into law, was an outspoken nativist of long standing. During his term as vice-president he had published an article, "Whose Country Is This?," in which he not only avowed Nordic supremacy but supported the notion that intermarriage between "Nordics" and other groups produced deteriorated offspring. Even the leaders of many of the longer-established immigrant groups supported the bill, as did many African-American leaders.

But the quota system set up in 1921 and 1924 was only the first step in 1920s immigration reform. The 1924 act called for a "scientific study" of the origins of the American people as of 1920, which would provide a new set of quota numbers beginning in 1929. This system, not the one established in 1924, should properly be what we now call the National Origins System. Based on that study, the president was to promulgate new quotas whose total was to be about 150,000, a reduction of about 30,000 spaces from the 1924 law. On the surface the procedure seemed fair, even scientific. The law provided that "national origin" percentages were to be calculated corresponding to "the number of inhabitants in continental United States in 1920 whose origin by birth or ancestry" was attributable to each nation. But the very next section of the law excluded from those calculations:

(1) any persons who were immigrants from the New World and their descendants;

(2) any Asians or their descendants;

(3) the descendants of "slave immigrants";

(4) the descendants of "American aborigines."

To work out the details of national origins, the American Council of Learned Societies appointed a committee of experts, including the father of immigration history, Marcus Lee Hansen. The committee complied with the racist notions of Congress and somehow "computed" the ethnic origins of the

American people as prescribed by the 1924 law. The result
was nearer to mysticism than social science. The expert
"guesstimate" was that persons whose ancestors were here before the Revolution constituted 43.4 percent of the eligible
1920 population—ignoring blacks, American Indians, and
Asians as the law stipulated—and that later immigrants and
their descendants constituted the rest. The practical results of
this estimate were significant: the quota for the United King-
dom rose from 34,007 (based on 2 percent of the 1890 census)
to 65,721. The quota for the Irish Free State was lowered from
28,567 to 17,853; Germany from 51,227 to 25,957; and those
from Sweden, Norway, and Denmark from a combined
18,803 to 6,872. The proposed quota numbers were approved
by the secretaries of state, commerce, and labor, and solemnly
proclaimed by President Herbert Hoover. An accompanying
statement noted his opposition to national origins—Hoover
knew enough statistics to know how shaky its empirical base
was—but came down "strongly in favor of restricted and selected immigration." Leaders among German, Scandinavian,
and Irish immigrants, who had largely supported restriction
thinking it would apply only to the newer immigrant groups,
complained about the lowered quotas—but to no avail.

   The short-term results of the 1924 law were not as drastic as
most restrictionists had hoped or as most history textbooks describe. During the first five years of the 1924 law, 1925–1930,
an average of 300,000 immigrants entered the United States
annually. This was sharply down from the 600,000 in each of
the first four years of the decade, or from the nearly 900,000
annually of the first decade of the century, but it was still
many more than restrictionists had hoped. The composition of
the immigrants, however, was markedly different from the
prewar period. In the decade before World War I, immigrants
from the New World had accounted for about 7 percent of the

total; in the six years after the act they constituted nearly half, 60 percent of them from Canada and most of the rest from Mexico. European immigration, a bare majority of the total after 1924, was dominated by British, German, and Irish migration, which aggregated 62 percent of quota immigration. During 1901–1910 these nations had accounted for only 13 percent of all immigration. Conversely, the share of other European nations was slashed. From 1925 to 1930, fewer than 90,000 Italians and 50,000 Poles entered the country. During 1921 alone, the last prequota year, 220,000 Italians and 95,000 Poles had come in. The following table shows the change in immigration flows in the 1920s.

IMMIGRATION IN THE 1920S BY REGION

Years	Total	Europe	%	Americas	%	Other	%
1921–24	2,344,599	1,541,008	65.7	730,393	31.1	73,198	3.1
1925–30	1,762,610	936,845	53.1	796,323	45.2	29,442	1.7

Average annual immigration, 1921–24: 586,150
Average annual immigration, 1925–30: 293,768

Source: Author's computation from INS data

One further significant change in immigration policy should be noted here, a change that took place at the end of the 1920s and was effected not by statute but by presidential executive order. Wishing to keep out many Mexicans, who could enter freely as nonquota immigrants, Herbert Hoover initiated a novel interpretation of the long-standing law forbidding entry of anyone "likely to become a public charge." When first placed on the statute books in 1891, the "LPC" clause had been aimed at persons who were obviously unlikely or unable to support themselves. For a long time the possession of $25 was sufficient to immigration inspectors. But in

1930 Hoover gave consular and immigration officials wide latitude in interpreting the LPC clause, and they used it, chiefly against Mexicans in the first instance but later in the 1930s to keep out poor refugees, especially Jews. While application was erratic, many would-be immigrants, quota and nonquota, had to produce affidavits promising support from some person or persons already in the United States in order to gain entry. As a September 1930 State Department press release explained: "If the consular officer believes that the applicant may probably be a public charge at any time, even during a considerable period subsequent to his arrival, he must refuse the visa." Thus this new interpretation was first used to reduce Mexican immigration and was then extended to the rest of the eligible world. Just as Chinese exclusion in 1882 had been the statutory hinge on which the golden door to America began to close, the application of the LPC clause to Mexicans in early 1929 was the administrative hinge for further narrowing. Once applied successfully to unpopular groups, each method of restriction was then applied to all groups.

While the 1920s legislation changed and restricted immigration patterns considerably, it was the Great Depression of the 1930s that brought immigration almost to a halt. In fact, during several years of the early 1930s, more persons left the United States than entered it, something that had not occurred since the great exodus of Loyalists at the end of the American Revolution.

It is difficult to overstate the prejudice against immigrants and other minorities that flowered in the 1920s among all classes in the United States. When the great liberal Supreme Court justice Oliver Wendell Holmes, Jr., spoke for a court majority in a case upholding a state's right to sterilize women regarded as mentally defective, his elegant decision argued that "the principle that sustains compulsory vaccination is broad enough to cover cutting the Fallopian tubes. . . . Three generations of imbeciles are enough." Although the "three generations" referred to a now-discredited study of poor white families, the overwhelming majority of such forced sterilizations were inflicted on minority women, African Americans and immigrants.

The political and cultural spokesmen of the decade, from presidents to motor magnates, spoke for an America that was rapidly vanishing. Albert Johnson, the prime mover of immigration restriction in the House of Representatives, spoke for many if not most Americans when he proclaimed, in 1927, that

> instead of a well-knit homogenous citizenry, we have a body politic made up of all and every diverse element. . . . Our capacity to maintain our cherished institutions stands diluted by a stream of alien blood. . . . It is no wonder, therefore, that the myth of the melting pot has been discredited. . . . The United States is our land. . . . The day of unalloyed welcome to all peoples, the day of indiscriminate acceptance of all races, has definitely ended.

Johnson, and most Americans of that era, would be astounded by the situation in the United States in the 1990s. Asians and persons of Hispanic descent and culture now dominate a growing immigration which in the 1990s ran at about 800,000 legal immigrants annually. Nor would they have been prepared to believe that American Indians and African Americans would become the subjects of much beneficent legislation, though neither group has ever received equal treatment from American society. A brief consideration of how these changes came about is the subject of the final chapter.

Epilogue: Toward Equality

THE GREAT DEPRESSION of the 1930s was one of the major turning points of United States history, an event that affected every aspect of American life. The two chief political antagonists of the decade, Herbert Hoover and Franklin Roosevelt, were each overtaken by the event. The more intellectually supple Roosevelt rode out the storm, but the economic crisis all but destroyed Hoover's popular reputation, even if almost sixteen million Americans voted for him in 1932, 39.9 percent of the total in the election that brought FDR and his New Deal to power. Some issues, like Prohibition, were simply blown away by the winds of change. The Eighteenth Amendment mandating Prohibition, which Hoover had called a "noble experiment," and which the pundit Walter Lippmann had gloomily prophesied was an unfortunate and permanent change, was repealed less than a year after FDR took office. Battles between "wets" and "drys," though they continued in some local arenas, never again enjoyed a national spotlight.

Unlike the Prohibition issue, deeply held prejudices about race, ethnicity, and religion did not fade away. They were, however, thrust further into the background as economic issues and political and social reform took center stage. Although almost every aspect of American life was changed by the time of Roosevelt's death in April 1945, continuity rather than change was the hallmark of most Americans' attitudes on race, ethnicity, and religion. Of the groups discussed in this book, there was a publicly proclaimed New Deal for only one—the Indians.

The Indian New Deal was explicit. The new commissioner of Indian affairs, John Collier, strongly supported by his boss, Interior Secretary Harold L. Ickes, was able to effect many of the reforms he had advocated in the 1920s. Collier skillfully took advantage of general New Deal programs as well as creating special ones for Indians. He managed to have special units for Indians included in many regular New Deal relief programs, such as the Civilian Conservation Corps. One historian has calculated that Indians received $45 million from various New Deal programs during just the first two years of the Roosevelt administration, at a time when the entire annual budget of the Bureau of Indian Affairs was less than half that. In addition, under Collier the BIA deliberately began to "Indianize" its bureaucracy by hiring more Indians. It also initiated an important program to encourage the production, exhibition, and sale of Indian arts and crafts, eventually creating a special Indian Arts and Crafts Board.

But the most significant New Deal reform was the Indian Reorganization Act of 1934. Although not nearly as thoroughgoing as Collier wished, the act nevertheless reversed many long-standing aspects of government treatment of and attitudes toward Native Americans. The chief change in attitude was an end, at least for a while, to the government's efforts to remold and "whiten" Indian culture. As an exponent of cultural pluralism, Collier believed Indians should govern themselves. Yet even he sometimes complained that the subjects of his reforms did not always want the "right" things or do things the "right" way.

The 1934 Reorganization Act wrote some of that philosophy into law. Under its provisions Indian tribes could constitute themselves into federal municipal corporations if they drafted formal constitutions and bylaws, which the act encouraged them to do. These newly formed tribal governments had powers that were often resented by their non-Indian neighbors, powers that were enhanced by the legal opinions of reform-minded lawyers. Interior Department Solicitor Nathan Margold, for example, revived Chief Justice John Marshall's 1831 ruling that Indian tribes were "dependent domestic nations" while ignoring Marshall's qualifying notion that they were "in a state of pupilage."

The new tribal constitutions prompted much criticism, chiefly:

(1) Since they followed Anglo-American legal norms, they were still "white man's law" rather than Indian law.

(2) Since many of them followed closely a "model constitution" drawn up by BIA lawyers, they often failed to respond to the varied conditions and cultures of modern American Indian life.

(3) Because the constitutions were written in English and followed Anglo-American practices, they tended to give power to the more acculturated "mixed bloods" as opposed to "full bloods."

Despite these and other criticisms—the most important of which was that Collier, like so many reformers in power, tended to be intolerant of whites or Indians who did not share his views—the Indian New Deal clearly marked a change in the relationship between Indian tribes and the federal government. Many Indians later remembered the 1930s not as a time of depression but as a time when more resources had been allotted to them. Still, American Indians remained the poorest, least educated, and shortest-lived group in American society.

No programs in the 1930s were aimed specifically at African Americans; neither Roosevelt or any of his lieutenants ever talked about a "New Deal for Negroes." The dominance of racist Southern Democrats in Congress even inhibited Roosevelt from pressing for such a modest civil rights measure as an antilynching bill. Yet by the time of the congressional elections of 1934 and the presidential election of 1936, most of the growing numbers of black voters had abandoned the Republican party and were voting for the Democrats, obeying the injunction of the black publisher-politician Robert Vann, who had urged blacks to "turn Lincoln's picture to the wall" because that debt had been paid.

The reason for their transfer of allegiance was not Vann's or anyone else's rhetoric but the tangible evidence of relief and in some cases jobs, even though African Americans did not get their fair share of federal programs. The most equitable programs, those run by relief administrator Harry L. Hopkins, tried with some success to give blacks about 10 percent of the jobs, which was roughly their proportion in the population. But even that standard discriminated, because poverty was not evenly distributed among the population, and black people had more than their share. Many private charities were less scrupulous. During the great Ohio Valley flood of 1937, for example, the American Red Cross gave smaller amounts of relief to Negro families than to white families of the same size. In Los Angeles at about the same time, the major Catholic charitable organization made the same kinds of discrimination between Mexican-American families and others. In each instance the rationale was that the families discriminated against were accustomed to being poor while many whites were not.

The Roosevelt administration did recognize some members of what W. E. B. Du Bois called the "talented tenth." Several dozen black men and a few black women received administrative appointments, most often as advisers on "Negro matters," in a great many federal departments and agencies. Many of these government officials met informally to exchange

ideas, and these meetings led to their being called, in the
African-American press at least, the "black cabinet," though
their jobs were not even at the subcabinet level. The most
prominent of these African-American New Dealers were
Mary McLeod Bethune, who directed the National Youth Administration's Division of Negro Affairs, and the economist
Robert C. Weaver, who served in a number of positions connected with housing and employment, and later became, in
Lyndon Johnson's administration, the first African-American
cabinet member. In addition, Franklin Roosevelt, and later his
wife Eleanor, often listened to black leaders and seemed sympathetic to their problems. And leading New Dealers could
make some spectacular gestures toward equality, such as stag-
ing a recital by the black contralto, Marian Anderson, at the
Lincoln Memorial after the Daughters of the American Revolution had denied her the use of its Constitution Hall for a
concert. As that incident underlines, Franklin Roosevelt's
Washington was still a segregated Southern city in which even
"black cabinet" members could not be served in most restaurants, could not try on clothes in those stores that welcomed
their business, and had to sit in the back of buses and streetcars.

Immigrants received no special New Deal, though largely
native-born Catholics and Jews were appointed to a distinctly
larger share of important positions than ever before. To be
sure, Secretary of Labor Frances Perkins was sympathetic to
immigrants and cleaned up some of the corruption and mis-
management in the immigration service. She also drew criticism for being too lenient in the enforcement of immigration
regulations. More important was that the consular service in
Roosevelt's administration simply continued the administrative restrictions adopted by Hoover's. In many cases they were

continued by the same officials. And although FDR quietly withdrew Hoover's executive order reinterpreting the LPC clause, most State Department officials continued to apply the more restrictive criteria. After Hitler's rise to power, this made it much more difficult for refugees, largely Jewish, to gain admission to the United States.

Although we tend to think of Roosevelt and Hoover, and their parties, as polar opposites, after 1920 the Democratic party's position on immigration was scarcely distinguishable from that of the Republicans. Although the 1928 Democratic candidate, Al Smith, was rightly regarded as a representative of the immigrant and urban masses, the Democratic platform that year pledged itself to preserving immigration restriction "in full force and effect," favoring more lenient provisions only for family reunification. Not one of the four platforms on which Franklin Roosevelt ran, from 1932 to 1944, contained a word about immigration, and there were no significant changes in immigration law until 1943. Candidate Roosevelt had made this clear in his 1932 Commonwealth Club address in San Francisco, arguing, in words reminiscent of Frederick Jackson Turner, that:

> Our industrial plant is built. . . . Our last frontier has long since been reached. . . . There is no safety valve in the form of a Western prairie. . . . We are not able to invite the immigration from Europe to share our endless plenty.

That is not to say that immigration policy would have been the same had Hoover been reelected. Hoover wanted immigration restricted even further, while the father of the New Deal was willing to stand pat. As FDR put it in another 1932 campaign address:

> [The President of the United States] says proudly that he has effectively restricted immigration in order to protect

American labor. I favor that; but I might add that in the enforcement of the immigration laws too many abuses . . .
have been revealed.

Roosevelt did not share Hoover's essentially nativist view of
most recent immigrants and their descendants. It is impossible
to imagine the Quaker engineer telling the Daughters of the
American Revolution, as FDR did, to "remember, remember
always that all of us, and you and I especially, are descended
from immigrants and revolutionaries." But for Roosevelt, immigration was apparently something that had happened in the
past. The New Deal did, however, treat resident aliens more
generously than its predecessor. It discontinued a Hoover administration "voluntary" repatriation program which had sent
perhaps half a million persons, including many American-
born children, back to Mexico, and it was less likely to deport
aliens. Deportations, which had risen steadily from 2,762 in
fiscal 1920 to 19,865 in 1933, dropped in the next year to fewer
than 9,000 and stayed at about that level for the rest of the
decade. Federal relief regulations insisted on the eligibility of
resident aliens, though local control of hiring usually discriminated not only against aliens but against persons of color regardless of citizenship.

The outbreak of World War II in 1939, and gradual U.S. involvement, had an even greater long-term effect on the American people than the depression. The war, not New Deal
reforms, finally ended the Great Depression and brought with
it a prosperity that eventually trickled down to some of the
most disadvantaged groups in American society. In addition,
since war and even the preparations for war called upon all
Americans to make sacrifices, it gave minority groups opportunities to make demands. Arthur Marwick's "participation

dimension" was much more evident in World War II America than in World War I. One reason was that American involvement was so much longer in World War II—almost four years as opposed to just over a year and a half. Another, probably more important, reason was that Roosevelt and many of his officials and advisers were committed to a more egalitarian society.

American Indians clearly benefited from the war. Donald Parman has argued that the war was "a central turning point for Indians in the West." Most obvious was the service of some 25,000 Indians in the armed forces, about 800 of them women. Most celebrated was the contingent of Navajo "code talkers" used by the Marines to baffle Japanese eavesdroppers. More important, the war opened off-reservation opportunities for Indians as never before and heightened such ongoing trends as migration to urban areas, a more sophisticated leadership, and a sharpened sense of goals and identity. But not all effects were positive. The tragic story of the Pima Ira Hayes, one of the group immortalized in the flag-raising on Iwo Jima, who died ten years later from exposure while intoxicated, is merely one example of failed integration or reintegration into civilian life which was the experience of a significant minority of American veterans.

For African Americans the war experience was more varied and complex. In 1941 a group of black leaders led by A. Philip Randolph threatened a March on Washington to demonstrate for equal rights unless President Roosevelt took tangible rather than symbolic steps toward racial equality. After negotiations with the president and later with some of his lieutenants and Eleanor Roosevelt, Randolph and his associates gained some of the concessions they wanted and called off the march. FDR agreed to issue an executive order creating a Fair Employment Practices Committee (FEPC) and to mandate an end to discrimination in civilian employment by the federal government and by private employers with defense (later war) contracts. Significantly Roosevelt did not accede to demands for integration in the armed forces, and the United States fought World War II with a Jim Crow military establishment. The FEPC was far from fully effective, but it did markedly increase defense and war employment for African Americans. Even more important, Randolph and his associates maneuvered the federal government into taking the first important steps toward racial equality since Reconstruction.

Other African-American protest was less focused, less dramatic, and without immediate tangible result. Much of the black press, for example, spoke of a "double V" campaign—victory over the Axis powers and victory over discrimination. But apart from the FEPC, little was accomplished in what one historian has called the "forgotten years of the Negro revolution." On the legal front the NAACP could report small victories in its long struggle against discrimination, but these gains seemed dwarfed by 1943 race riots in Harlem and Detroit.

For most immigrants and their children, even those whose origins were in eastern and southern Europe, the war years involved a greater recognition of their contributions to American society, as they too benefited from the participation dimension. For Jewish Americans there was a distinct decline in overt anti-Semitism once America went to war against Hitler. The historian Glen Jeansonne has argued that:

> There are several reasons for the . . . decline of . . . anti-Semitism in general. The most important factor was World War II. It may have been respectable to oppose the foreign policies of the Roosevelt administration from an isolationist viewpoint prior to the war, but continued isolationist hyste-

ria, frequently mixed with anti-Semitism, was considered unpatriotic if not actually treasonous in wartime.

It must also be noted that in the late 1920s a reaction had begun in the scientific community against the "scientific racism" that had stained so much scholarship. Crucial, perhaps, was the work in anthropology of Franz Boas and his students Alfred Kroeber, Ruth Benedict, and Margaret Mead. Their antiracist ideas, which stressed the essentially unitary nature of humankind, began to permeate the social sciences in the 1930s and 1940s, and to prevail in the humanities in the 1950s and 1960s.

During World War II even those whose birth or roots were in the lands of America's European enemies, Germany and Italy, were included in the wartime consensus that regarded white persons as, in Philip Gleason's phrase, "Americans all." Unlike World War I propaganda, which stigmatized Germans as "Huns," World War II propaganda stressed the differences between "good" and "bad" Germans. Coincidentally, the U.S. "crusade in Europe" was led by a general with a German name, Eisenhower. Although unnaturalized persons of German and Italian birth were officially classified as enemy aliens, few were deprived of their liberty. Most Italian-born aliens, in fact, were officially removed from that status by presidential proclamation on Columbus Day 1942, just before the off-year congressional elections.

But the Roosevelt administration, though clearly antifascist, did little for the victims of fascism, apart from destroying it. Although the president was no anti-Semite and appointed more Jews to public office than all his predecessors combined, his State Department was infested with nativists and anti-Semites, including his friend Assistant Secretary of State Breckinridge Long, who made it difficult for most refugees to

gain asylum in the United States. Congress was adamantly opposed to refugee immigration from the European continent
and even thwarted attempts to bring in refugee children, most
of whom would have been Jewish. Yet after the war broke
out, Congress made the entry of British children easier. Some
of Roosevelt's administrative rulings allowed many refugees
to stay in the United States, and very late in the war he created
the War Refugee Board. But Walter Mondale's judgment,
many years later, that the United States and other nations of
the West "failed the test of civilization" insofar as refugees
from Nazism were concerned, is now accepted by most historians.

Unlike German and Italian Americans, Japanese Americans suffered dearly for the actions of their country of origin.
More than two months after the attack on Pearl Harbor, the
federal government began the worst mass violation of Americans' civil liberty in the twentieth century. More than 120,000
Japanese Americans, more than two-thirds of them native-
born citizens, were incarcerated in ten desolate concentration
camps. Ironically, the effective instrument was the same as
that used to establish the FEPC, a presidential executive order.
Although the government, in a series of actions between 1948
and 1988, eventually apologized and furnished monetary re-
dress to the survivors of America's concentration camps, during the war there was little protest against the plight of these
Asian Americans. The Supreme Court, traditionally reluctant
to impede presidential power in wartime, refused to abolish
the camps in the Japanese-American cases of 1943 and 1944.

At the same time, curiously, the long history of anti-Asian
legislation began a reversal. In 1943 Congress, at FDR's urging, repealed the fifteen laws that had effected Chinese Exclusion, allowed Chinese aliens to become naturalized citizens,
and permitted a token quota—105 slots per year—to Chinese

immigrants. Just as the Chinese Exclusion Act of 1882 was the hinge on which the golden door of immigration began to swing closed, its repeal in 1943 was the hinge on which it began to open wider. It was not concern for the fewer than 100,000 Chinese Americans that triggered the change, of course, but a desire to recognize a wartime ally. Once an exception had been made for Chinese, other exceptions followed: Filipinos and "natives of India" in 1946, and all other Asians in 1952.

The immediate postwar years brought no dramatic changes in the status of minority groups; in many ways their status seemed to be lowered. Congress, in a conservative reaction, sought to repeal many of the New Deal's Indian policies and "free" Indians from federal control, a policy abetted by the Truman and Eisenhower administrations. At the same time improving economic conditions benefited many Indians, and the migration of Indians to cities was accelerated. Indians also won civil rights victories. In 1948 Indians in New Mexico and Arizona received the right to vote, which meant they could also receive state old-age assistance, aid to the blind, and aid to dependent children. By 1953 Congress had enabled Indians to purchase liquor and carry firearms off the reservations. In 1946 Congress passed compulsory school attendance laws for school-age Indians, and in 1950 it began to subsidize school districts with Indian pupils. In 1945 more than 60 percent of all Indian children in school attended segregated BIA schools; by 1970 nearly 70 percent of such children attended public schools.

For African Americans, continued migration north and west was perhaps the salient feature of the immediate postwar years. No civil rights legislation emerged from Congress, but President Harry S. Truman did order the integration of the armed forces, an integration that was largely effected during

the Korean War, 1950–1953. It was the Supreme Court of the
United States that triggered what some have called the "Second Reconstruction" with its unanimous May 1954 decision in
Brown v. Board of Education, holding that "segregation in public education . . . is a denial of equal protection of the laws" as
guaranteed in the Fourteenth Amendment and thereby unconstitutional. The Court, led by Chief Justice Earl Warren,
explicitly reversed the "separate but equal doctrine" laid down
in *Plessy v. Ferguson* and helped trigger decades of fruitful activism. The Court's decision did not come out of the blue;
rather it was a link in a major chain of cases, most of them
brought by the NAACP and its separate legal arm, which
transformed the legal position of African Americans and
eventually touched almost every aspect of American life.

Changes affecting immigration came even more quickly.
The discovery of the Nazi death camps pricked many American consciences, and a bipartisan political effort to admit relatively large numbers of displaced persons from Europe,
beyond quotas, was ultimately successful. When bills for the
admission of a total of 415,000 displaced persons passed Congress in 1948 and 1950, it was clear that the 1920s quota system
was dead, though it would technically linger on until 1965.
Die-hard congressmen, who often chaired crucial congressional committees, insisted on at least a pretense that the quota
system was intact, and they got it. Quotas were simply mort-
gaged! As a result, to cite an extreme example, so many Lat-
vians were admitted to the United States that the annual
quota for Latvia of 286 persons was quickly used up (mort-
gaged) to the year 2274. A conservative Congress rejected Truman's proposals for a more liberal immigration statute, but in
the McCarran-Walter Immigration and Nationality Act of
1952 it fulfilled Charles Sumner's dream and made naturalization color-blind. Remaining bars to Asian ethnic groups

were dropped, so that members of all racial and ethnic groups were now eligible for both immigration and naturalization.

But the McCarran-Walter Act also maintained the worst kinds of ethnic biases as it pretended to continue the moribund quota system. It also added stringent political tests for all who sought to enter the United States, even as visitors, and was otherwise redolent of the worst aspects of the cold war. How did such a statute at such a time significantly liberalize naturalization policy? The answer has little to do with immigration and naturalization policies per se, but rather with the fact that such policies are usually influenced by foreign policy. When the United States had an isolationist foreign policy, an immigration and naturalization policy that kept most of the peoples of the world from coming to America was entirely appropriate. But in the post–World War II world, in which the United States sought a kind of hegemony and the leadership of the "free world," such policies were no longer appropriate.

The cold war also, at least in a minor way, abetted the black 'revolution. The State Department never showed significant concern about segregation until African diplomats, whose votes in the United Nations General Assembly were important to American foreign policy, began to complain about the demeaning and discriminatory treatment they received in and around Washington and elsewhere in the United States.

Domestic politics, of course, played its usual important role in social change. Since the 1950s the legal and social positions of Native Americans and African Americans have undergone dramatic changes, changes due both to the consciences of some of the majority, and, even more important, to the increased activism of more and more minority individuals and organizations. Slogans such as "Black Power" and "Red Power" frightened not only many members of the white majority but also some old-style leaders of African Americans and Native Americans. What the newer and younger activists wanted was more self-determination, more grassroots control, and less direction from the federal government, while at the same time calling for greater federal support.

While the changes in the situation of Native Americans and African Americans can best be described as evolution, many recent changes in immigration appear to be revolutionary. Thanks in large part to the relatively liberal Immigration Act of 1965, the patterns of immigration to the United States have been turned on their head. Dominated by Europeans before 1924, immigration in recent decades has been dominated by immigrants from Asia and Latin America, who have constituted more than 80 percent of recent immigrants. If we were able to calculate illegal immigrants as well, the figure would probably amount to more than 90 percent. Before the quota system was enforced, Italians, Poles, and eastern European Jews dominated; after the 1965 act, Chinese, Filipinos, and Mexicans are the largest groups.

Even the opposition to immigration has undergone a sea change. In debates over immigration in the 1920s and 1930s, nativists nakedly stated their prejudices; by 1965 most of those resisting a more liberal policy claimed to be unprejudiced. In the 1965 Senate debates, Democrat Sam Ervin of North Carolina, the chief advocate of the status quo, insisted that the McCarran-Walter Act was not discriminatory but rather was "like a mirror reflecting the United States, allowing the admission of immigrants according to a national and uniform mathematical formula recognizing the obvious and natural fact that those immigrants can best be assimilated into our society who have relatives, friends, or others of similar background already here."

What Ervin and others never admitted was that the "mirror" was badly distorted, like those at amusement parks, and reflected not 1960s population but that in the 1920 census. Ervin and other nativists were outvoted. The 1965 act abolished the quota system and made family unification the keystone of immigration policy. Immigration has swelled in recent decades and will probably total at least 8 million persons for the 1990s, approaching the level reached before World War I. Present-day nativists, such as members of FAIR (Federation for American Immigration Reform), who view the numbers of contemporary immigrants with alarm, fail to note that while the 8-million-plus immigrants of the first decade of this century came to a country of some 90 million persons, those in the 1990s come to one of more than 250 million. Thus the incidence of foreigners in American society—about 8 percent in the 1990 census—is still well below late-nineteenth- and early-twentieth-century norms of about 14 percent.

Refugee policy has also changed markedly in recent decades. Before and during World War II the United States had no separate policy: refugees were treated like other immigrants. But beginning with the Displaced Persons acts of 1948–1950, special ad hoc provisions were made for different groups of refugees, culminating in the idealistic Refugee Act of 1980, the only truly significant piece of immigration legislation since 1965. It came at a time when the so-called compassion level in the United States was relatively high, and it was so uncontroversial that it passed the Senate by a vote of 85 to 0, cosponsored by the normally antagonistic Edward M. Kennedy and Strom Thurmond. The bill showed that, four decades after Congress and the Roosevelt administration had turned a deaf ear to persons fleeing from Hitler, a positive refugee policy had become part of the American consensus. It established a new American right, the right of asylum for persons who fitted the refugee definition even if they were, as often has been the case, already in the United States illegally.

In assessing how contemporary American society treats its ethnic and racial "others," it is important to take into account both how much improvement there has been, and how much still needs to be improved. Many observers have noted a decline in the degree of egalitarianism felt by most Americans since 1965, the annus mirabilis of late-twentieth-century liberalism. Anti-immigrant sentiments are rife and exacerbated by right-wing politicians and talk-show hosts. In the mid-1990s public opinion polls consistently showed that some 65 percent of Americans felt there were too many immigrants, both legal and illegal, and that something ought to be done about it. Similarly a popular anti-Indian backlash has developed in much of the West and Midwest in reaction to increased Indian tribal authority, court protection of Indian fishing rights, tax exemptions, and gambling concessions.

Although, as Andrew Hacker has argued, "from slavery to the present, the nation has never opened its doors sufficiently to give black Americans a chance to become full citizens," most white Americans—and particularly white male Americans—believe that for at least the last generation blacks have been given more than a fair chance and at least equal opportunity, if not outright advantages. What many persons see as the unfairness of affirmative-action and set-aside programs, designed to close the economic gap between minority Americans and whites, has produced a backlash, largely against blacks.

Whether these and other signs of late-twentieth-century discontent are omens of an impending reversal of policy, or whether they are minor regressions toward former attitudes, is not for the historian to say. What the historian can see is that the commitment to equality has both waxed and waned in the American past, and there is every reason to expect that such a pattern will continue in the twenty-first century.

A Note on Sources

RATHER THAN ATTEMPT to list all the sources, primary and secondary, I have consulted in a professional lifetime of reading and research, this note will indicate, by chapter, some important relevant books and articles and indicate the source of long quotations, except for those whose source is given in the text or is obvious.

PROLOGUE: CHINESE EXCLUSION, 1882

The seminal work on nativism is John Higham, *Strangers in the Land: Patterns of American Nativism, 1860–1925* (New Brunswick, N.J., 1955), while Tyler G. Anbinder, *Nativism and Slavery: The Northern Know Nothings and the Politics of the 1850s* (New York, 1992) is the best account of its main pre–Civil War manifestation. For the anti-Chinese movement, Elmer C. Sandmeyer, *The Anti-Chinese Movement in California* (Urbana, Ill., 1939; 2nd ed. 1991) is still valuable but should be supplemented with Stuart C. Miller, *The Unwelcome Immigrant* (Berkeley, 1969) and Alexander Saxton, *The Indispensable Enemy* (Berkeley, 1971). For the Chinese themselves, the best single work is Sucheng Chan, *This Bittersweet Soil: The Chinese in California Agriculture, 1860–1910* (Berkeley, 1986), and the broader story can be followed in Roger Daniels, *Asian America: Chinese and Japanese in the United States Since 1850* (Seattle, 1988). The study of modern indentured labor begins with Hugh Tinker, *A New System of Slavery: The Export of Indian Labour Overseas, 1830–1920* (London, 1974); it should be supplemented with Walton Look Lai, *Indentured Labor, Caribbean Sugar: Chinese and Indian Migrants to the British West Indies, 1838–1918* (Baltimore, 1993). Two brilliant works analyze the mutual impact of Chinese immigrants and American law: Charles J. McClain, *In Search of Equality: The Chinese Struggle Against Discrimination in Nineteenth-Century America* (Berkeley, 1994) and Lucy E. Salyer, *Laws Harsh as Tigers: Chinese Immigrants and the Shaping of Modern Immigration Law* (Chapel Hill, 1995).

Quotations: [p. 4] The Peruvian newspaper is cited from Watt Stewart, *Chinese Bondage in Peru* (Durham, N.C., 1951), p. 105.

[p. 5] Sir John Bowring quoted from Robert L. Irick, *Ch'ing Policy Toward the Coolie Trade, 1847–1878* (Taipei, 1982), p. 27.

[p. 8] Caleb Cushing cited from Reginald Horsman, *Race and Manifest Destiny: The Origins of American Racial Anglo-Saxonism* (Cambridge, Mass., 1981), p. 253.

[p. 13] Senator Morton in U.S. Congress. Senate. *Misc. Document 20* (Washington, D.C., 1877), p. 4.

[p. 15] Selig Perlman, *A History of Trade Unionism in the United States* (New York, 1922), p. 62.

[p. 17] Victor and Brett de Bary Nee, *Longtime Californ': A Documentary Study of an American China* (New York, 1973), p. 63.

All three quotations on p. 19 are from Lawrence B. Davis, *Immigrants, Baptists and the Protestant Mind in America* (Urbana, Ill., 1973), pp. 42–43, 44, 83.

1. THE UNITED STATES IN THE GREY NINETIES

The most single useful book on late-nineteenth-century America is Carl N. Degler, *The Age of the Economic Revolution, 1876–1900* (Glenview, Ill., 1973). Charles W. Calhoun, ed., *The Gilded Age: Essays on the Origin of Modern America* (Wilmington, Del., 1996) contains stimulating essays with up-to-date bibliographies. Robert Wesser, *A Response to Progressivism: The Democratic Party and New York Politics, 1902–1920* (New York, 1986) contains good brief analyses of the ideology and tactics of both major parties. William T. Hagan's essay "United States Indian Policies, 1860–1900," in William C. Sturdevant, ed., *Handbook of North American Indians,* vol. 4 (Washington, D.C., 1988) is the best brief introduction to a complex subject. For details consult the relevant documents in Wilcomb E. Washburn, ed., *The American Indian and the United States: A Documentary History* (New York, 1973). Edward L. Ayres, *The Promise of the New South* (New York, 1992) is a good analysis of the region in which most African Americans lived. Herbert Shapiro, *White Violence and Black Response: From Reconstruction to Montgomery* (Amherst, Mass., 1988) is comprehensive and authoritative. August Meier, *Negro Thought in America: Racial Ideologies in the Age of Booker T. Washington* (Ann Arbor, 1980) is indispensable for African-American intellectual history. Arnold M. Paul, *Conservative Crisis and the Rule of Law: Attitudes of Bar and Bench, 1887–1895* (Ithaca, N.Y., 1960) is important for understanding the milieu in which legal decisions were shaped. Roger Daniels, *Coming to America: A History of Immigration and Ethnicity in American Life* (New York, 1990) is a general history. Barbara Miller Solomon, *Ancestors and Immigrants: A Changing New England Tradition* (Cambridge, Mass., 1956) is good for its treatment of the Immigration Restriction League and the attitudes that nurtured it.

Quotations: [p. 21] Turner's essay, "The Significance of the Frontier in American History," first appeared in the *Annual Report* of the American Historical Association for 1893; the second essay, "Western State-Making in the Revolutionary Era," in the *American Historical Review* 1 (1895), 71.

[p. 22] Henry Steele Commager, *The American Mind: An Interpretation of American Thought and Character Since the 1890s* (New Haven, Conn., 1950), p. 41.

[p. 29] Black Elk, *Black Elk Speaks* (Lincoln, Nebr., 1988), p. 276.

[p. 31] Robert A. Trennert, Jr., *Alternative to Extinction: Federal Indian Policy and the Beginnings of the Reservation System, 1846–51* (Philadelphia, 1975), pp. 194–195.

[p. 33] Booker T. Washington, *Up from Slavery: An Autobiography* (New York, 1903), p. 220.

[p. 34] Du Bois cited from Ayres, *New South*, p. 71.

[p. 40] Massachusetts. Bureau of Statistics of Labor. *Twelfth Annual Report* (Boston, 1981), p. 489.

2. THE LIMITS OF PROGRESSIVISM

Important interpretations of progressivism include George E. Mowry, *The California Progressives* (Berkeley, 1951); Albert D. Chandler, "Origins of Progressive Leadership," vol. 8, Appendix III, in E. E. Morison, ed., *The Letters of Theodore Roosevelt* (Cambridge, Mass., 1954); Richard Hofstadter, *The Age of Reform: From Bryan to F.D.R.* (New York, 1955); and Robert H. Wiebe, *The Search for Order, 1877–1920* (New York, 1967). For Indians, Donald L. Parman, *Indians and the American West in the Twentieth Century* (Bloomington, Ind., 1994) is an excellent guide. Blue Clark, *Lone Wolf v. Hitchcock: Treaty Rights and Indian Law at the End of the Nineteenth*

Century (Lincoln, Nebr., 1994) illuminates the tangled state of law affecting Indians. For black leadership, see Louis R. Harlan, *Booker T. Washington*, 2 vols. (New York, 1972, 1983). Charles Flint Kellogg, *NAACP: A History of the National Association for the Advancement of Colored People* (Baltimore, 1967) covers the period through 1920. The most important single volume on Irish immigration is Kerby P. Miller, *Emigrants and Exiles: Ireland and the Irish Exodus to North America* (New York, 1985). No such study exists for Germans, but see Kathleen N. Conzen, "Germans," in Stephan Thernstrom, ed., *The Harvard Encyclopedia of American Ethnic Groups* (Cambridge, Mass., 1980). For a fascinating account of cultural transfer and adaptation, see Robert A. Orsi, *The Madonna of 115th Street: Faith and Community in Italian Harlem, 1880–1950* (New Haven, Conn., 1985). A classic account of eastern European Jews is Moses Rischin, *The Promised City: New York's Jews, 1870–1914* (Cambridge, Mass., 1962). Leonard Dinnerstein, *Antisemitism in America* (New York, 1994) is the best account. For anti-Japanese activities, see Roger Daniels, *The Politics of Prejudice: The Anti-Japanese Movement in California and the Struggle for Japanese Exclusion* (Berkeley, 1962).

Quotations: [p. 49] Letter to Chief No Shirt, May 18, 1905, in Morison, *Letters of Theodore Roosevelt*, VI, 1185–1188.

[p. 54] Anonymous, "The Atlanta Massacre," *Independent*, October 4, 1905, as reprinted in Allen D. Grimshaw, ed., *Racial Violence in the United States* (Chicago, 1969), p. 45.

[p. 54] As quoted by William English Walling, "The Race War in the North," *Independent* (September 3, 1908), pp. 529–534.

[p. 61] David M. Kennedy, et al., *The Brief American Pageant*, 3rd ed. (Lexington, Mass., 1993), II, 357.

[p. 61] U.S. Immigration Commission, *Reports of the Immigration Commission* (Washington, D.C., 1911), I, 24.

[p. 70] Michael La Sorte, *La Merica* (Philadelphia, 1985), p. 148.

3. World War I and the Ambiguities of Nationalism

David M. Kennedy, *Over Here: The First World War and American Society* (New York, 1980) is a good survey. Stephen L. Vaughn, *Holding Fast the Inner Lines: Democracy, Nationalism, and the Committee on Public Information* (Chapel Hill, 1980) is a thorough account of American war propaganda. Arthur Marwick's theoretical notions can be conveniently seen in his "Problems and Consequences of Organizing Society for Total War," in N. F. Dreiszinger, ed., *Mobilization for Total War: The Canadian, American and British Experience, 1914–1918, 1939–1945* (Waterloo, Canada, 1981). Michael L. Tate, "From Scout to Doughboy: The National Debate Over Integrating Indians into the Military, 1891–1918," *Western Historical Quarterly* 17 (October 1986) relates Indian military service. The best work on black migration is James R. Grossman, *Land of Hope: Chicago, Black Southerners, and the Great Migration* (Chicago, 1989). For Brownsville, see Ann J. Lane, *The Brownsville Affair: National Crisis and Black Reaction* (Port Washington, N.Y., 1971); for Houston, see Robert V. Haynes, *A Night of Violence: The Houston Riot of 1917* (Baton Rouge, La., 1976); and for East St. Louis see Elliott Rudwick, *Race Riot in East St. Louis, July 2, 1917* (Carbondale, Ill., 1964). For Americanization generally, see Philip J. Gleason, "American Identity and Americanization," in Thernstrom, *Harvard Encyclopedia of American Ethnic Groups*. Frederick C. Luebke, *Bonds of Loyalty: German-Americans and World War I* (De Kalb, Ill., 1974) is outstanding. For the assault on civil liberties generally, see Paul L. Murphy, *World War I and the Origin of Civil Liberties in the United States* (New York, 1979).

Quotations: [p. 83] Charles C. Teague, *Fifty Years a Rancher* (Los Angeles, 1944), p. 141.

[p. 84] Sells cited in Jared Gardner, " 'Our Native Clay': Racial and Sexual Identity and the Making of Americans in *The Bridge*," *American Quarterly* 44 (March 1992), 27–30.

[p. 86] U.S. Congress. House, *East St. Louis Riots: Report . . .* , 65th Cong., 2nd Sess., House Document No. 1231 (Washington, D.C., 1917).

[p. 87] "Why We March," NAACP leaflet as quoted in Charles M. Christian, *Black Saga: The African American Experience* (Boston, 1995), p. 311.

[p. 91] Cubberly quoted from Bernard J. Weiss, ed., *American Education and the European Immigrant* (Urbana, Ill., 1982), p. xiii.

[p. 91] S. Breckenridge and E. Abbott, *The Delinquent Child and the Home* (New York, 1912), p. 63.

[p. 92] Cuomo cited in Italian American Historical Association, *The Urban Experience of Italian Americans* (New York, 1975), p. 6.

[p. 92] E. A. Ross, "Racial Consequences of Immigration," *Century Magazine* 87 (February 1914), 617–619.

[p. 92] Constantine Panunzio, *Immigrant Crossroads* (New York, 1927), p. 250.

[p. 95] Felsenthal cited in Arthur A. Goren, "Jews," in Thernstrom, *Harvard Encyclopedia of American Ethnic Groups*, p. 579.

4. POSTWAR PASSIONS

William Preston, Jr., *Aliens and Dissenters: Federal Suppression of Radicals, 1903–1933* (Cambridge, Mass., 1963) is a seminal work. John D. Hicks, *Rehearsal for Disaster: The Boom and Collapse of 1919–1920* (Gainesville, Fla., 1961) is useful on the economic dislocations of the period. There are many studies of the riot and of African-American Chicago; for the latter, see Allan H. Spear, *Black Chicago: The Making of a Negro Ghetto, 1890–1920* (Chicago, 1967); for the former, see William M. Tuttle, *Race Riot: Chicago in the Red Summer of 1919* (New York, 1970). The Tulsa riot is analyzed in Scott Ellsworth, *Death in a Promised Land: The Tulsa Race Riot of 1921* (Baton Rogue, La., 1982). Walter White's account appeared in *The Nation* (June 29, 1921). Felix Frankfurter, *The Case of Sacco and Vanzetti: A Critical Analysis for Lawyers and Laymen* (Boston, 1927) is still worth reading. Joseph P. O'Grady, ed., *The Immigrants' Influence on Wilson's Peace Policies* (Lexington, Ky., 1967), summarizes the activities of a number of groups; for Jews, see Jacob Rader Marcus, ed., *The Jew in the American World: A Source Book* (Detroit, 1996), p. 178ff.; for Greeks, see Theodore Saloutos, *A History of the Greeks in the United States* (Cambridge, Mass., 1964).

Quotations: [p. 105] Material on NAREB is from David H. McKay, *Housing and Race in Industrial Society: Civil Rights and Urban Policy in Britain and the United States* (Totawa, N.J., 1977), p. 53.

[p. 106] Chicago Commission on Race Relations, *The Negro in Chicago: A Study of Race Relations and a Race Riot* (Chicago, 1922), passim.

[p. 112] For McKay and his poem, see Claude McKay, *Selected Poems* (New York, 1953).

[p. 114] J. Saunders Redding, *On Being Negro in America* (Indianapolis, 1951), p. 127.

[p. 119] George J. Sánchez, *Becoming Mexican American: Ethnicity, Culture and Identity in Chicano Los Angeles, 1900–1945* (New York, 1993), p. 133.

5. THE TRIUMPH OF NATIVISM

Hawley's interpretation is *The Great War and the Search for a Modern Order: A History of the American People and Their Institutions, 1917–1933* (New York, 1979), and Dumenil's is *The Modern Temper: American Culture and Society in the 1920s* (New York, 1995). Robert K. Murray, *The Politics of Normalcy: Governmental Theory and Practice in the Harding-Coolidge Era* (New York, 1973) is a useful brief account of the politics of the era. For John Collier's early career, see Lawrence C. Kelly, *The Assault on Assimilation: John Collier and the Origins of Indian Policy Reform* (Albuquerque, N.M., 1983). The best work on the Klan in the 1920s is Kenneth T. Jackson, *The Ku Klux Klan in the City, 1915–1930* (New York, 1967). For details of Japanese exclusion, see Daniels, *Politics of Prejudice*.

Quotations: [p. 128] Army War College report as cited by Doris Kearns Goodwin, *No Ordinary Time: Franklin and Eleanor Roosevelt: The Home Front in World War II* (New York, 1994), pp. 160–170.

[p. 129] Hughes cited in Bradford Luckingham, *Minorities in Phoenix: A Profile of Mexican American, Chinese American, and African American Communities, 1860–1992* (Tucson, Ariz., 1994), p. 142.

[p. 133] Consular reports as cited in Higham, *Strangers in the Land*, p. 309.

[p. 138] Sánchez, *Becoming Mexican American*, p. 131.

[p. 138] Carr letter to Johnson, December 4, 1920, as cited in Patricia R. Evans. " 'Likely to Become a Public Charge': Immigration in the Backwaters of Administrative Law, 1882–1933" (unpublished Ph.D. dissertation, George Washington University, 1987).

[p. 139] The quoted provisions are from Section 11, subdivision "d" of the 1924 immigration act, 43 *Stat.* 153.

[p. 143] Holmes cited by Mark Haller, *Eugenics: Hereditarian Attitudes in American Thought* (New Brunswick, N.J., 1963), p. 139.

[p. 143] Albert Johnson, as cited in Roger Daniels, *Racism and Immigration Restriction* (St. Charles, Mo., 1974), p. 10.

EPILOGUE: TOWARD EQUALITY

Two excellent recent surveys of the Roosevelt era are Anthony J. Badger, *The New Deal: The Depression Years, 1933–1939* (New York, 1989) and John W. Jeffries, *Wartime America: The World War II Home Front* (Chicago, 1996). For African Americans in the New Deal era, Nancy Weiss, *Farewell to the Party of Lincoln: Black Politics in the Age of FDR* (Princeton, N.J., 1983) and Harvard Sitkoff, *A New Deal for Blacks: The Emergence of Civil Rights as a National Issue* (New York, 1978) are standard works. Sitkoff's *The Struggle for Black Equality, 1954–1992* (New York, 1993) is a useful summary. George W. Martin, *Madam Secretary: Frances Perkins* (Boston, 1976) contains a good account of the corruption in the immigration bureaucracy. Alison R. Bernstein, *American Indians and World War II: Toward a New Era in Indian Affairs* (Norman, Okla., 1991) is a thorough treatment; Cletus E. Daniel, *Chicano Workers and the Politics of Fairness: The FEPC in the Southwest, 1941–1945* (Austin, Tex., 1991) is the best work on the FEPC. Three excellent studies of race riots in the Roosevelt era are Cheryl L. Greenberg, *"Or Does It Explode?"* (New York, 1991); Dominic J. Capeci, *The Harlem Riot of 1943* (Philadelphia, 1977); and Dominic J. Capeci and Martha Wilkerson, *Layered Violence: The Detroit Rioters of 1943* (Jackson, Miss., 1991). For a fascinating account of science and racism, see Daniel J. Kevles, *In the Name of Eugenics: Genetics and the Uses of Human Heredity* (Berkeley, 1986). On the changing nature of "Americanism," Philip Gleason, "Americans All: World War II and the Shaping of American Identity," *Review of Politics* 43 (1981), 483–518, is excellent. George E. Pozzetta, "'My Children Are My Jewels': Italian-American Generations During World War II," in K. P. O'Brien and L. H. Parsons, eds., *The Home-Front War: World War II and American Society* (Westport, Conn., 1995), pp. 62–82, is a sensitive account of immigrant angst. For Jewish refugees in wartime, see Richard Breitman and Alan M. Kraut, *American Refugee Policy and European Jewry, 1933–1945* (Bloomington, Ind., 1987) and Sharon R. Lowenstein, *Token Refuge: The Story of the Jewish Refugee Shelter at Oswego, 1944–1945* (Bloomington, Ind., 1986); their postwar treatment is analyzed in Leonard Dinnerstein, *America and the Survivors of the Holocaust* (New York, 1982). The Japanese incarceration is treated in Roger Daniels, *Prisoners Without Trial: Japanese Americans in World War II* (New York, 1993). General immigration policy since World War II is analyzed in David M. Reimers, *Still the Golden Door: The Third World Comes to America* (New York, 2nd ed., 1992), and Asian immigrants and their children are described in Harry H. L. Kitano and Roger Daniels, *Asian Americans: Emerging Minorities* (Englewood Cliffs, N.J., 2nd ed., 1992).

Quotations: [pp. 149–150] Commonwealth Club speech in Samuel I. Rosenman, ed., *The Public Papers and Addresses of Franklin D. Roosevelt* (New York, 1938), 1928–1932 volume, p. 750; Boston speech, October 31, 1932, in *ibid.*, p. 854; DAR speech in *ibid.*, 1938 volume, p. 258.

[p. 151] Parman, *Indians and the American West*, p. 183.

[p. 153] Glen Jeansonne, "Combatting Anti-Semitism: The Case of Gerald L. K. Smith," in David A. Gerber, ed., *Anti-Semitism in American History* (Urbana, Ill., 1987), p. 153.

[p. 158] Ervin is quoted from U.S. Congress. Senate. Subcommittee on Immigration and Naturalization of the Committee on the Judiciary. *Immigration*. Hearings. 89th Cong., 1st Sess. (Washington, D.C., 1965), pp. 63–67.

[p. 160] Andrew Hacker, *Two Nations: Black and White, Separate, Hostile, Unequal* (New York, 1992), p. 23.

Index

A NOTE ON THE AUTHOR

Roger Daniels was born in New York City and grew up in various parts of the United States, largely in the South. He served in the merchant marine during World War II and in the army during the Korean War. He was educated at the University of Houston and at UCLA, where he earned a Ph.D. in history. He has written widely on matters of race and ethnicity, including, most recently, *Coming to America: A History of Immigration and Ethnicity in American Life* (1990) and *Prisoners Without Trial: Japanese Americans in World War II* (1993). A past president of the Society for Historians of the Gilded Age and the Progressive Era and of the Immigration History Society, he is now Charles Phelps Taft Professor of History at the University of Cincinnati.